Vegan Ethics

AMORE—Five Reasons to Choose Vegan

Lisa Kemmerer
tapestryofpeace.org

Dedication

For all who live on this planet now and in the future.

All proceeds from this book return directly to Tapestry (tapestryofpeace.org). Our work is only possible with the generous support of readers like you.

Acknowledgments

This book is the work of professor emeritus Dr. Lisa Kemmerer at Tapestry (tapestryofpeace.org). Many thanks to readers who offered suggestions, especially Matthew Halteman and my brother, Ed Kemmerer.

Cover design
Lisa Kemmerer

Contents

INTRODUCTION

Food and eating are basic, central, and important to our lives. While food is a biological necessity, the place and importance of food extends far beyond physical needs. We usually eat at least a few times every day; some people are perpetual snackers. We eat for pleasure, nutrition, and to waylay stress. Individuals also have particular food patterns such as morning drinks, reward snacks, after-exercise meals, and comfort foods. Many people enjoy food preparation and sharing food; most people look forward to the next snack or meal. Food claims a notable portion of each day, from earning what we need to buy food, to shopping for what we need (or gathering foods directly from the earth), to prep and cooking, and finally, the meal itself.

Partaking of food is often a social activity—so much so that it is difficult to imagine a gathering without drinks and snacks or a shared meal. Every culture has food specialties and long-held food traditions. Families develop much-loved recipes and treasured food traditions. Sharing treasured foods or recipes is often part of friendship, and some of these foodways have traveled from faraway homes, whether an Asian veggie stir-fry, North American bagel, or European tomato pasta. Sharing food can be a way of spending time with others, of stopping the perpetual doing of life independently in order to spend time directly with our closest contacts. Food is central to our lives as individuals, families, and communities.

> Prepping a meal for someone is akin to telling him or her a story about who you are, where you come from, and where you hope to go in the future. (Christopher Carter, Ph.D., The Spirit of Soul Food)[1]

Anything as important and social as food and meals is certain to have a list of protocols. From an early age we learn table-manners, including expectations for day-to-day meals and additional manners for eating in public, eating with guests, and for eating special meals such as holiday feasts. We are taught when we may start eating, how to properly move food around the table and serve from shared dishes, how to politely put food in our mouths and chew, what to do (and not to do) while sharing time at the table, and how to properly complete and exit the eating ritual.

Because food entails many resources, is wrapped in treasured and ancient traditions, and is part of our everyday lives and daily habits, it is bound to be laden with ethical implications and religious guidelines. It is also true that anything as ubiquitous, habitual, and laden with tradition is food is likely to slide under the moral wire—*eating is almost always a matter of habit and not a matter of reflective choice.* One of the most obvious signs of this are localized foods in very globalized economies. People in south India tend to eat a lot of lentils, people in Korea tend to eat a lot of rice, people in Nigeria tend to eat a lot of casava, and not even one of these foods is a core staple across North America. Wheat is common in Iraq, corn in Columbia, and potatoes in Bolivia, and each of these foods is common in North America. We eat what is available, we eat what is affordable, but most fundamentally, we eat what our families taught us to eat. And we rarely consider the ethics of what we eat.

The foods we choose to eat are likely the most important moral/ethical choice that we make, partly because we make this choice every day, several times a day. The word "choice" is critical in ethics: Those who do not have a choice are not morally culpable. That said, if you are reading this, you are almost surely among those who select what you eat.

Eating is ethics in action. The most basic moral decision that we make when we choose what we will eat is whether to eat anymal[1] products—flesh, dairy, or eggs. There are five weighty concerns that go with choosing to be an omnivore (plant foods and anymal products) or vegetarian (no flesh, but plants, dairy, and eggs). The acronym AMORE ("love" in Italian) helps to recall five moral concerns that point to a vegan diet:

1. **A**nymals
2. **M**edical
3. **O**ppression
4. **R**eligion
5. **E**nvironment

Each of these moral concerns shapes one of the five chapters of this book.

---

[1] Animals and Religion uses the term "anymal" (a contraction of "any" and "animal," pronounced in English as "any" and "mul") to avoid using "animals" incorrectly, as if humans were not animals. (In this writing, quotations from other writers maintain their incorrect use of "animal.") Current alternatives to this incorrect usage are cumbersome and dualistic, including "nonhuman animal" and "other-than-human animal."

Anymal indicates all individuals of a species other than that of the speaker/author/signer. In other words, if a human being uses this term, they refer to all species except *Homo sapiens*, but if a chimpanzee signs "anymal," they indicate all species (including human beings) except their own. Therefore, when used by the author of this book, "anymal" indicates all living beings except human beings. (See Kemmerer, "Verbal Activism: 'Anymals'" at http://lisakemmerer.com/publications.html (Society and Animals 14.1, 2006: 9-14).

1. ANYMALS

Every year, worldwide, uncounted hundreds of billions of fishes and shellfishes, 8 billion chickens, 214 million turkeys, 124 million pigs, 36 million bovines (cattle), 23 million ducks, and 7 million sheeps are killed for omnivores—human beings who eat anymal products as well as plant foods.[2] Anymals (individuals from every species outside of my own)—suffer physically and mentally because they are exploited for food, and with the exception of sealife (which can be killed at any age) they are killed in early adolescences—except those few who are exploited for reproduction, in which case they live to be young adults. In choosing to buy dairy, eggs, or flesh, omnivores are responsible for funding—and therefore bringing about—all of this suffering and premature death for these billions of individuals.

Standard practices worldwide for anymals exploited in food industries, including fishing, aquaculture, anymal agriculture, and hunting, raise considerable moral concerns. Fishes are not protected by the most basic welfare laws in any nation, but that said, illegal practices are exposed every time undercover investigators in any nation penetrate the increasingly thick walls of anymal agriculture facilities that breed, raise, or kill anymals for human consumption. Even the most minimal welfare laws are rarely practiced or enforced, and at any given time, it is safe to assume that no one will see how anymals are treated in the industrial farming system, where anymal lives are valued only by their dollar value in the food market. Hunters and fishers—who choose to kill anymals for food when they would not need to do so—also cause suffering and premature death, and fund ecosystem manipulations through state agencies that cater to hunters and fishers.

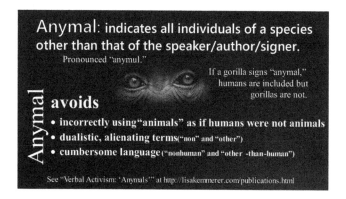

Anymal: indicates all individuals of a species other than that of the speaker/author/signer.
Pronounced "anymul."

If a gorilla signs "anymal," humans are included but gorillas are not.

Anymal avoids
- incorrectly using "animals" as if humans were not animals
- dualistic, alienating terms ("non" and "other")
- cumbersome language ("nonhuman" and "other -than-human")

See "Verbal Activism: 'Anymals'" at http://lisakemmerer.com/publications.html

This chapter mentions only a small portion of the moral concerns associated with eating anymal products, focusing on just a few species. For more information on any one species or on species not covered here, see anymal activist websites in the nation where you live. Please be sure to view undercover footage.

Fishes

The only reason fishing is regarded as a wholesome activity and not a cruel past-time is because people cannot hear the fish screaming in pain. . . . fighting for life. Fish feel pain. Fishing is cruelty to animals. (Michael Gurwitz, attorney on the U.S. Section of Agriculture, *Fish Feel*)[3]

Fishes are vertebrates with a complex nervous system. Anatomical, pharmacological, and behavioral data, as well as our understanding of evolution and neurophysiology, indicate that fishes are sentient.[4] It "is unthinkable that fish do not have pain receptors; they need them in order to survive."[5] It also seems unthinkable that catch-and-release is considered a sport, when it causes so much unnecessary suffering and loss of life. Free ranging anymals who have been maimed (by sport fishers) will struggle to recover and are much less likely to survive. A Study on striped bass, "one of the most prized species in the Chesapeake Bay and along the Atlantic Coast," revealed that "the number of fish that died after being handled by recreational anglers . . . exceeded the number they actually kept."[6]

When hauled out of their natural environment by a hook embedded in their delicate mouths, fish thrash, writhe, and struggle in an attempt to escape. They gasp desperately in the air, unable to breathe out of water, as they slowly begin to suffocate. Like any other animals, their struggles indicate an aversion to pain and a strong will to survive. (*Voices For Animals*)[7]

Because they are sentient, fishes ought to be protected by animal welfare laws, but they are not protected anywhere in the world—and there is no quick death for sealife caught in the fishing industry. Fishing methods entail slow death by suffocation after being caught by hooks or nets. Also morally problematic, fishing methods are indiscriminate. Hooks pierce any living being that grabs the bait and nets collect anything within their margins.

Fishing's indiscriminate methods result in bykill or bycatch, often referred to as "trash," which includes unintended and endangered species. Morally speaking, this is an extremely important complication of consuming fishes: Those who eat fishes are not only responsible for funding the death of that which they eat, but of all bykill that goes with that particular choice of foods.

Bykill kills hundreds of billions of sealife annually. Bykill slows the recovery of over-fished species and endangers otherwise healthy underwater populations. For example, blue and white marlins (billfishes), though "identified as overfished," are frequent bykill victims.[8] In the Potomac River, herring have failed to recover from overfishing, and more river herring are caught as bykill "than the 1 million pounds caught annually in the few remaining [herring] fisheries."[9] Herring fisheries also contribute to severely depleted populations of cod, hake, haddock, and others who live near the ocean floor.[10] As a result, "river herring and shad populations have dwindled to less than 5 percent" of what they once were.[11]

Shrimp nets are the worst bykill offenders. The Food and Agriculture Organization (FAO) of the United Nations estimates that shrimp haul anywhere in the world consists of 85% bykill.[12] Sea turtles are all protected, but shrimp fishing destroys more turtles than all other human activity combined,[13] working against the many efforts to protect and restore these vastly diminished species. Those who eat shrimp may as well eat endangered sea turtles.

Shrimp fishing amounts to only 2 percent of the global wild seafood catch, but is responsible for 30 percent of all the bycatch in the world's fisheries. In some tropical shrimp fisheries, the bycatch is fifteen times the quantity of the shrimp caught. Thailand, the largest source of imported U.S. shrimp [has] a bycatch ratio of 14:1. (Peter Singer and James Mason in *The Way We Eat*)[14]

Bykill is also "the primary threat" to several species of endangered marine mammals.[15] Cetaceans are common "trash" on the hooks of longlines, including pilot whales, false killer whales, Risso's dolphins[16] and pseudorcas (also dolphins).[17] Less than 20 years ago, estimates indicated that some 6,000 cetaceans (including whales, dolphins, porpoises) and pinnipeds (both seals and sea lions) were drowning in nets every year.[18] "A new study estimates that about 80,000 cetaceans are swept up every year [just] by" gill nets fishing for tuna in the Indian Ocean.[19] Gill nets, used to catch such fishes as tuna, salmon, cod, and pollock, have all but eliminated the vaquita (a porpoise), the world's most endangered cetacean. Twenty years ago, there were an estimated three hundred individuals remaining; now there are only about twenty individuals left on the planet[20] and illegal fishing continues to kill vaquitas at an alarming rate—any rate is alarming with so few individuals remaining.[21] (The vaquita's desperately low numbers continue to decline because people continue to buy the fishes that are brought in by illegal fishing, and in fact there is no way for consumers to tell the difference Consumers who buy fishes have no way of knowing that the product they support with their purchase was fished illegally and is drives the vaquita ever closer to extinction.

Commercial fishing destroys an estimated 300,000 seabirds annually. Nearly half of the earth's endangered seabirds are threatened because of commercial fishing.[22] Longline fishing is "a critical threat to albatrosses and large petrels."[23]

Because fishing drowns, injures, and/or stresses those caught, bykill mortality rates are 90-100 percent even for those who survive long enough to be released back into the water.[24] For example, when turtles are caught on hooks and survive long enough to be freed, the physiological stress of the experience affects their "ability to feed, swim, [and] avoid predators."[25] Because they cannot breathe underwater, most birds and marine mammals who are caught on hooks or nets drown before they can be released.

Sea life is not counted by the individual, but by the ton. Fisheries and fish-eaters destroyed roughly 197 million tons (179 million metric tons) of life *just as bykill* in 2018.[26] Decade after decade hooks pull in billions of [tons of] living beings that are considered trash by the industry. Those who purchase the flesh of fishes drive the fishing industry and fund sufferings, loss of life, species depletions, and species extinctions caused by the fishing industry.

Fish are fast learners with long-term memories and a keen sense of time. They recognize other individuals, can keep track of complex social relationships, and work cooperatively with other species. Fish are inquisitive, perceptive, and personable.

Globally, an estimated one to three trillion wild-caught fishes and 37-120 billion farmed fishes are killed commercially for food each year. Hundreds of millions more are killed for "sport" each year in the U.S. alone. *(Fish Feel)*[27]

Cows and Steers

Like humans, goats, dogs, and other mammals, cows only lactate to feed their young—after they give birth. Cow's produce milk (and hens lay eggs) as part of their basic, biological functioning—not because they are well cared for or contented. Even the most miserable woman, if provided with adequate food and water, will ovulate (pass eggs) and lactate (produce milk) after birth. Common sense tells us that the same is true for cows (and chickens).

In order for cows to produce milk, they must be pregnant, so those in the dairy industry repeatedly, forcibly, artificially impregnate cows as soon as they are old enough to conceive. Mothers exploited by the dairy industry carry their young for ten months, but their calves are taken from them after birth. Cows, like most mammals who nurse their young, have a strong mothering instinct, and try desperately to defend and protect their calves. They bawl for days after their babies have been taken.

On my first morning, I stood in the freezing pens with tiny babies who [had been taken from their mothers and who] looked absolutely shattered; still wet with afterbirth, bloody umbilical cords dangling. . . .

Mothers were birthing outside my window and I was listening to their labour pains all night, then watching them loving and cleaning their babies until my partner came with the tractor and the cage and took those babies away from them forever. . . . I couldn't believe what I had been so complicit in, and what evil I had been closing my eyes and heart to. (Jessica Strathdee writing of what she witnessed while living and working on a dairy farm)[28]

Motherless calves in the dairy industry are sold for veal, an industry that was created to take advantage of these little living by-products of dairy. The veal industry, which thrives because human beings consume milk, cheese, ice cream, and yogurt, confines and kills one million calves every year, either immediately after birth or four to six months later. Those who live four to six months are confined in tiny pens and fed on a milk substitute that is deficient in iron and fiber. (Human beings buy their mother's milk.) This deprivation creates the anemic, light-colored flesh that is prized by those who purchase veal.

As for those calves who are kept for the dairy industry, their tails are "docked" with blades that cut through flesh, vertebrae, and tendons. The buds where their horns would normally grow are seared from their skulls. Anesthesia is never used for these unnecessary surgeries, which are performed for the convenience and economic interests of the dairy industry. When buds were seared from the heads of these little calves, an observer wrote that despite bound mouths, the calves bellowed, "wheezed, frothed and strained."[29]

After birthing and losing their calves, the bereaved mothers endure mechanized milking for ten out of twelve months of the year (including seven months of their nine-month pregnancies). Genetic manipulation, dietary controls, and synthetic hormones cause extraordinary and unnatural milk output—fifty pounds of milk per day. While cows normally produce just over two tons of milk per year, cows in the dairy industry provide as much as thirty tons of milk annually—enough for ten calves. With this extreme and unnatural production, the udders of one in five cows are painfully infected so that pus oozes from their udders and invariably mixes with the milk. United States regulations permit "750,000 cells of pus" while the European Union allows for 200,000 cells of pus in any given milliliter of milk that is sold, including organic milk.[30]

On sanctuaries, cattle can live upward of twenty years, but cows kept for dairy are so physically and emotionally exhausted by reproductive exploitation that they are "spent" and sent to slaughter after just four or five years of perpetual pregnancy, birthing, and milking. Most cows are pregnant when they arrive at the slaughterhouse, and many arrive so exhausted and demoralized that they are unable or unwilling to stand or walk. They are dragged from trucks by tractors and chains.

In the beef industry, cows and steers (castrated males) suffer third-degree burns when they are branded; males are also castrated. These procedures are completed without anesthesia—or any other medications.

At six or seven months of age, the young are taken from their mothers and transported to feedlots, where they are crowded into manure-packed pens with as many as 10,000 other youth, to be fattened for slaughter. On feedlots, cows and steers are fed growth-promoting hormones and unnaturally rich diets to double their weight in the few months before their slaughter.

Every year some 166,000 cows and steers are dead on arrival at the slaughterhouse.[31] The mothers, who bawl loudly for days after their young are taken, are shipped to slaughter after about six years of perpetual birthing and raising of young. Slaughtering methods are shaped and driven by economic factors—the quicker each anymal is killed, the higher the owner's profit margin. Cows and steers are killed at a rate of about 250 individuals per hour. At such speeds, the process by which they are meant to be rendered unconscious or lifeless is often incomplete and entirely ineffective. Undercover footage shows cattle kicking, struggling, and fully conscious as they are hoisted onto the slaughter dis-assembly line and cut into pieces. On viewing such footage, it is difficult to imagine the pain these terrified cows and steers must be feeling, or what they might be thinking.

The cattle were supposed to be dead before they got to Moreno. But too often they weren't.

"They blink. They make noises," he said softly. "The head moves, the eyes are wide and looking around." Still Moreno would cut. On bad days, he says, dozens of animals reached his station clearly alive and conscious. Some would survive as far as the tail cutter, the belly ripper, the hide puller. "They die," said Moreno, "piece by piece." (Interview with slaughterhouse employee, Ramon Moreno, in *The Washington Post*)[32]

Poultry

There are roughly 20 billion chickens in the world. Roughly ten billion are hatched each year in the United States, where more than 95 percent of these birds will be factory-farmed, living out their short lives in tight confinement, unable to satisfy even their most basic and natural urges—like the urge to fully extend and stretch our limbs.

Some thirty million chickens are exploited as "laying hens." Compare this to any numbers given for human sufferings and death—which are never standard practice, but are instead remembered with great sadness, often as a moral outrage. But factory farm conditions are simply a given for billions of anymals around the world all day and all night long.

In the egg industry, some two hundred million newly hatched male chicks are also discarded every year in chippers or via gas. In the United States, male chicks are often chucked straight into garbage bins, where they dehydrate or asphyxiate. Eyewitness accounts describe struggling, peeping chicks crushed and dismembered by metal blades. Their little fluffy bodies, when ground to oblivion, are sold as fertilizer or as feed for farmed anymals who would normally eat only plants and plant products.

Chickens kept for their reproductive eggs live in extremely tight confinement, crowded into cages with other hens. To reduce injuries caused by stress in overcrowded conditions, female chicks destined for the egg industry are "debeaked"—the tips of their beaks are sliced off with a hot blade that cuts through bone, cartilage, and soft tissue that is rich with nerve endings. All factory farmed poultry are debeaked without anesthesia shortly after hatching, and as a result, a predictable percentage of these fuzzy little chicks bleed to death or die of shock.

At eighteen weeks of age, four or more hens are stuffed into a crowded 1.5-square-foot cage, though any given hen's wingspan is roughly 2.5 feet. These crowded cages are piled one on top of the other in giant sheds. Hens exploited for eggs remain in these cages until they are sent to slaughter.

Hens have a strong nesting and mothering urge, but they must lay eggs on the floor of the wire cage where they live, and then watch their eggs roll onto a conveyor belt to be taken to consumers. Factory-farmed hens are never able to build a nest, sit on their eggs, or tend young—or, for that matter, walk on the ground or feel sunshine on their backs.

Each factory farmed hen produces upwards of 250 eggs in a year, though their wild counterparts lay only about twenty eggs in the same time span. Egg production quickly peeks and then naturally declines over the following months. The hens then go through what is called molt and start a new egg cycle, each cycle lasting about a year, and each producing slightly fewer eggs than the previous year. To maximize profits, hens exploited for eggs are put through "forced molt," forcing them to prematurely start a new laying cycle.[33] Forced molt entails being deprived of food and kept in total darkness for one to two weeks, sometimes longer. Some hens lose more than 25 percent of their body weight during forced molt. Five to ten percent of the hens die during forced molt, but since they are worth nothing to the egg industry when they are between laying cycles, forced molt is economically advantageous. Hens who survive and recover enter a second egg cycle.

Hens in the egg industry are comparatively likely to suffer from "cage-layer fatigue" due to calcium deficiency caused by excessive egg production. (Calcium is used to create eggshells.) Due to calcium deficiency, these hens can no longer stand on their painful and fragile legs, easily suffer fractures, and are likely to become "egg bound" and die because they are too malnourished to expel yet one more egg.[34] Hens in the egg industry are also more likely to suffer a prolapse (the uterus is expelled along with an egg) and egg peritonitis (an inflammation), none of which receive veterinary care because hens are considered cheap and expendable in the egg industry, and veterinarians are expensive. Most factory farmed hens have sores from rubbing against the cage wires, many develop cancers, severe liver and kidney disease, and infectious bronchitis (from living in their own excrement); due to calcium deficiency, broken bones are more likely and more common, but the veterinarian is not summoned for any of these painful conditions. In fact, it is unlikely that anyone would even notice such common ailments and injuries on an egg farm.

It is not cost-effective to send comparatively small and scrawny "layers" to slaughter. In the United States, millions of these "spent" hens are thrown (alive) into woodchippers—a "common industry practice."[35] In the European Union they are gassed, a death that generally takes a couple of minutes, but which is less shocking to any observers. Whatever method is used, "layer" hens are killed when they are in their adolescence.

Chickens at sanctuaries might live for fifteen years, but factory-farmed hens are killed just one year after they hatch.

In the hope of staving off heart attacks, strokes, and cancers that are medically linked with consuming red flesh, many consumers have shifted to "white" flesh, which has benefited the broiler industry. Hens are crowded by the thousands into warehouses that hold as many as 100,000 birds bound for human consumption. The floors of these giant crowded sheds quickly become covered with excrement, which causes chronic lung ailments in hens. They also develop blisters, ulcers, and burns on their feet, legs, and breasts from standing and lying in their nitrogen-rich waste. (Nitrogen causes burns.) Crowded in giant barns, hens also suffer from heat prostration, infectious diseases, and cancers.

They also suffer from heart failure. Hens raised for human food reach four pounds—slaughter weight—in just six weeks, growing twice as fast, and twice as large, as chickens did just a few decades ago. Their bones and hearts cannot support such unnatural weight gain and perish from heart disease. Those who live to be slaughtered are likely to experience chronic pain in the last weeks of their short lives.

Forty-five days after they hatch, "broiler" hens reach "market weight" and are grabbed—by a wing, leg, or by their heads as they scramble frantically for safety—and stuffed into crates that are stacked on trucks. These terror-stricken, plump birds, with weak hearts and fragile bones, suffer dislocated and broken hips, legs, and wings. Because they are handled roughly and tossed into wire cages as quickly as possible, some suffer from internal hemorrhaging and heart attacks, others suffocate. Once loaded with hens, these transport cages are stacked on open trucks that sometimes travel at eighty miles per hour in subzero temperatures or are parked at waystations in extreme heat while drivers eat or sleep. Needless to say, some freeze to death while others die of heat stress. Roughly 20 million chickens are dead when the transport trucks unload at the slaughterhouse.[36]

Roughly one million factory-farmed chickens are killed each hour for human consumption. In the United States, ninety percent of land anymals killed for food are birds, but federal laws fail to regulate the slaughter of fowl. At the slaughterhouse, hens are dumped onto conveyor belts. Some land on the floor and are crushed by machinery or die from starvation or dehydration. Those on the belt are hung by their legs, upside down, in metal shackles, to be transported along the disassembly line.

Along the way, their heads are supposed to touch an electrified basin of water to immobilize the birds for killing. Many move their heads to avoid the water. The water basin is designed to immobilize the hens, but many remain conscious (and suffering).

After passing the electric water basin, the chicken's throats are supposed to be cut, either by hand or with a mechanical blade, but slaughter lines run up to 8,400 chickens per hour. At such rates, accuracy is the exception rather than the rule. Nonetheless, the birds are soon submerged in scalding water (to loosen feathers)—those whose throats were not slit (or were not slit properly)—millions annually—are boiled alive.

My experience with chickens for more than twenty years has shown me that chickens are conscious and emotional beings with adaptable sociability and a range of intentions and personalities. If there is one trait above all that leaps to my mind in thinking about chickens when they are enjoying their lives and pursuing their own interests, it is cheerfulness. Chickens are cheerful birds, quite vocally so, and when they are dispirited and oppressed, their entire being expresses this state of affairs as well. The fact that chickens become lethargic in continuously barren environments, instead of proving that they are stupid or impassive by nature, shows how sensitive these birds are to their surroundings, deprivations and prospects. Likewise, when chickens are happy, their sense of wellbeing resonates unmistakably. (Karen Davis, Ph.D., founder of United Poultry Concerns)[37]

Pigs

One hundred million pigs are raised and slaughtered every year for human food. More than 95 percent of today's pigs are raised on factory-farms, where they spend their short lives in crowded little concrete pens. Pigs on factory farms stand and sleep in their own feces, urine, and vomit. Undercover footage shows that they even live amid the corpses of other pigs.

Sows who are exploited for reproduction are put through a continuous cycle of forced impregnation, tightly confined birthing, and forced nursing. Nursing young are then taken to be more quickly fattened for slaughter. Five days after piglets are taken, a sow is again forcibly, artificially impregnated. Sows endure at least two pregnancies, births, and nursing cycles each year, generally birthing more than twenty piglets annually. When a sow is no longer considered productive (after birthing four to seven families), she is sent to slaughter, usually at about four years of age, though pigs can live beyond fifteen years.

During their four months of pregnancy, breeding sows are sometimes isolated in gestation crates—small metal pens (two feet wide) with cement floors. Gestation crates hold pigs in one place, prevent pigs from turning around or lying down comfortably. These crates, widely recognized as excessively cruel, have been outlawed in a handful of nations and U.S. states, but where permitted, are still standard practice on many pig farms.

When it is time for them to give birth, sows are often transferred to similarly cramped farrowing crates with concrete or metal floors. These tiny pens, also illegal in a handful of nations and states, are equipped with bars that prevent mothers from reaching their piglets, but which allow the young to suckle (or chew) freely on the mother's teats. This results in lacerations and infections on the sow's teats. Short chains or rubber straps sometimes further immobilize the mother so that she cannot escape what must be a painful nursing experience. The goal is to fatten piglets for market as quickly as possible.

Psychological suffering is often recognized as more intense and unbearable than physical suffering. In their natural environment, sows build a nest with leaves or straw before giving birth, but they cannot build nests in barren concrete pens. As they approach term, sows sometimes resort to neurotic coping behaviors, repeatedly and desperately trying to build a nest, moving their heads backward and forward pointlessly in a rhythmic fashion, or gnawing on surrounding metal bars. Overcrowding and boredom add to their vexation, and pigs sometimes become aggressive. This has led to the practice of chopping off tails and cutting teeth on piglets (without anesthesia). From an economic point of view, it is cheaper to dock tails and cut teeth than it is to provide adequate space.

Factory-farmed sows, repeatedly impregnated and perpetually confined, suffer from weak bones and muscles, heart problems, and frequent urinary tract infections. Concrete floors and lack of exercise lead to crippling leg disorders, arthritis, and obesity. Respiratory disease is common, and in the United States, seventy percent suffer from pneumonia. But veterinarians are expensive in comparison with the value of any one pig, and the pigs are not valued as living beings or individuals, but by the pound.

Normally piglets nurse for about fifteen weeks, but factory-farmed piglets are taken from their mothers after just two or three weeks of nursing. The piglets are weaned in crowded, concrete "nursery" pens, where they are surrounded by metal bars and have little more than one square yard of floor space per pig. They are slaughtered at about six months of age.

About 330,000 pigs die in transit to slaughter every year.[38] As with all factory-farmed anymals, when shipped to slaughter, pigs are not provided food, water, or protection from extreme weather. "Downer" pigs, who either have lost the will to stand or are physically unable to do so, are dragged from transport trucks with tractors and chains.

Once inside the slaughterhouse, pigs are shackled and hoisted by one hind leg, usually causing massive damage to the leg from which they hang. They are moved along the line to the "blood pit," where a worker cuts (or attempts to cut) the struggling pig's throat—sometimes at the remarkable rate of 900 pigs per hour. Again, there is little of precision in this process. Undercover video shows conscious pigs along the processing line, hanging upside down by one leg, with workers try to "stick" the kicking and struggling pig. Sometimes the unfortunate pig remains conscious all the way to the scalding tank, to be boiled alive.

> When allowed to live without torment, pigs snuggle, they dream, they sing to their young . . . . Just like dogs, they are social, smart creatures. Pigs are clean animals who, in natural conditions, love bathing in water or mud and are careful not to soil areas where they eat or sleep. (Animal Liberation Queensland)[39]

Pigs are intelligent and social. Those who tend a pig or two at home say that they make great pets—that they are similar to dogs. Those who know pigs love them dearly and are horrified at the thought of their beloved pet suffering and dying in the meat industry.

Hunting

> There is no nutritional need to consume flesh—venison or beef or chicken. People who are genuinely committed to minimizing suffering must ask a broader question: Do I need to eat animal products? Those who

---

> sincerely wish to reduce suffering (and protect
> ecosystems)—will hunt out potatoes and
> pickles rather than deer and ducks. For those
> sincere in their quest for a compassionate diet,
> the answer is vegan, not venison. (Lisa Kemmerer,
> Ph.D., Eating Earth: Environmental Ethics and Dietary
> Choice.)[40]

Obviously, choosing to buy eggs, dairy, or any type of flesh contributes to extreme suffering and premature death—as does hunting. Hunting and fishing terrorize anymals, cause drawn-out deaths from wounding and suffocation, and kill anymals who might otherwise enjoy many years of life. Because fishes are covered above, this portion will focus on hunting.

Hunters cannot and do not shoot accurately each time they pull the trigger. Those who are wounded are left to die slowly in the elements, perhaps of infection, blood loss, or shock, perhaps because they cannot escape predators or forage. Estimates indicate that as many as 30 percent of those shot are left wounded.[41] Bored with the ease of shooting anymals with guns, some switch to mechanized bows, but bow hunters, who send an average of 14 arrows per kill, have a wounding rate of greater than 50 percent.[42] Hunting also leaves wild communities in dread and terror—anxious, frightened, and "emotionally scarred."[43]

Wounding is inevitable for bird hunters. Fowl are gunned down with shotguns that scatter pellets, hitting wings and legs, grazing heads and breasts. While "bird dogs" retrieve some of those who are wounded, many fall too far outside the dog's range, or they fall where a dog cannot reach them. Others are simply too healthy to be caught, but over time, they die of infections, blood loss and shock, predator attacks, starvation, and exposure.

Miseries caused by sport hunters (and fishers) are multiplied by government programs that manipulate ecosystems on behalf of those who hunt and fish for sport. Government agencies systematically destroy free ranging anymals on behalf of hunters and fishers (and anymal agriculture), targeting predators such as wolves, coyotes, and cougars. These programs kill tens of thousands of individuals, altering ecosystems. Because they use traps and poisons, they harm and kill endangered and threatened species, as well as cats and dogs.[44] As people shift to a plant-based diet, government agencies will be forced to manage free ranging anymals on behalf of the vast majority—hikers and kayakers and bird watchers—those who prefer to see all types of anymals and intact ecosystems.

Some hunters justify their sport as a means of low-cost sustenance, but hunting is comparatively expensive: buying firearms or bows, ammunition or arrows, boots and clothes, license and permit, gear upgrades and replacements, a worthy vehicle and gasoline, and the cost of butchering and preparing the corpse if not done at home—it all adds up quickly. Travel expenses have become a significant portion of the cost of hunting, including the cost of buying, insuring, and maintaining (or renting) a suitable vehicle. Deer hunters pay about forty dollars per pound for venison once all of the costs have been figured in. And of course, all of these expenses do not guarantee even one meal.[45]

In a bowhunting magazine, one hunter admits: "Nobody hunts just to put meat on the table because it's too expensive, time consuming, and extremely inconsistent"—hunters shoot at anymals "because it's fun!"[46] Honesty, while sometimes disturbing, can provide clarity. Perhaps the best proof that hunters simply enjoy shooting anymals is that they kill tens of millions of mourning doves and squirrels, a couple million woodchucks, hundreds of thousands of prairie dogs and crows, and thousands of skunks every year.[47] Ecosystems would benefit from a law requiring that hunters eat what they kill.

Gardening presents an attractive alternative to hunting. Growing a garden provides time in the outdoors, plenty of one-on-one family-time, and costs very little. Community gardens are available in many locations for free or for very little. Economically, bulk staples are even better than gardening for price per pound. It is pretty easy to find large bags of rice, pasta, or potatoes that can be cooked up with big bags of beans, lentils, or tofu. Human beings have depended on these foods for centuries, and these choices avoid the moral quagmire of overtly terrifying and killing anymals, of sometimes leaving them wounded, and of paying the government to kill thousands of anymals, altering ecosystems. Gardening and buying bulk staples are cheaper, more dependable sources of sustenance, and free of the moral quagmire of killing for sport.

Hunting is no longer motivated by hunger. Twenty-first century sport hunters are never without a full belly, even after investing tens of thousands of dollars on brand-new 4x4 pickups, motorboats, RVs and of course the latest high-tech weaponry.[48] (Jim Robertson in Exposing the Big Game)

Summary

To cause suffering or premature death—particularly when we might choose a different path—is a particularly serious moral concern. Choosing foods that cause egregious suffering and death (usually at a very young age) to trillions of anymals each year, when we might just as well choose vegan, seems so counterintuitive morally as to be both perplexing and deeply disturbing.

RESOURCES

Please be sure to search YouTube for footage from undercover investigations at anymal agriculture facilities.

For more on anymal suffering in the food industry, see
- Animal Aid. https://www.animalaid.org.uk/the-issues/our-campaigns/animal-farming/undercover-investigations/.
- Animal Equality. https://animalequality.org/investigations/.
- Animal Outlook. https://animaloutlook.org/investigations/.
- Farm Sanctuary. https://www.farmsanctuary.org/why-farm-animals/
- People for the Ethical Treatment of Animals. https://www.peta.org/investigations/.
- Mercy for Animals. https://mercyforanimals.org/investigations/.

For more on farmed birds see United Poultry Concerns:
- https://www.upc-online.org/battery_hens/
- https://www.upc-online.org/broiler/
- https://www.upc-online.org/turkeys/

For more on cows and the dairy industry, see
- Milk Future Museum. https://www.milkfuture.com/
- Animal Equality. "Suffering in the Dairy Industry. https://animalequality.org/issues/dairy/
- PETA. "The Dairy Industry." https://www.peta.org/issues/animals-used-for-food/factory-farming/cows/dairy-industry/
- Mothers Against Dairy. https://mothersagainstdairy.org/
- "Cow Longevity Economics: The Cost Benefit of Keeping the Cow in The Herd."

http://www.milkproduction.com/Library/Scientific-articles/Management/Cow-longevity-economics-The-cost-benefit-of-keeping-the-cow-in-the-herd/

- "To Keep or to Cull."
https://afs.ca.uky.edu/content/keep-or-cull
- "Dynamics and Strategies for Culling in a Dairy Herd."
https://afs.ca.uky.edu/Dynamics-and-Strategies-for-Culling-in-a-Dairy-Herd
- "Culling Decisions and Dairy Cattle Welfare During Transport to Slaughter in the United States."
https://www.frontiersin.org/articles/10.3389/fvets.2018.00343/full
- "Facts on Veal Calves."
https://www.hsvma.org/facts_veal_calves#.YGtELz9MHIU

For more on diet, ethics, and hunting and fishing, see

- Kemmerer, Lisa. *Eating Earth: Environmental Ethics and Dietary Choice.* Oxford: Oxford UP, 2014.
- Kheel, Marti. *Nature Ethics.* Rowman & Littlefield, 2007.

2. MEDICAL

Eating anymal products is linked with a number of life-altering and life-destroying medical problems. By affecting individual health, these medical problems also affect others—partners, children, and friends are harmed when those they care about (or depend on) have a paralyzing stroke, are bed-ridden with cancer, or die suddenly from a heart attack. Our health effects not only family and friends, but through loss of productivity and elevated medical costs, our communities. For example, somewhere between 200,000 and 500,000 coronary artery bypass surgeries are performed every year in the United States, each costing about $123,000.[49] Medical advice for preventing coronary artery bypass is dietary—adopt a whole-foods, plant-based diet.[50]

The World Health Organization and the Center for Disease Control (and many other sites) report that some of the world's top killers and most significant health threats for human beings, especially in wealthier nations, are linked to the consumption of anymal products—dairy, eggs, and flesh, including fish flesh—including heart disease, strokes, and cancers.[51] In contrast, not even one community health threat has been traced back to a vegan diet. Instead, studies show that the presence of contented anymals in our lives is medically advantageous, lowering heartrate and helping to release stress.[52] This lowered heartrate is merely a measurable symptom of a larger truth—when we care for anymals kindly and responsibly, our lives are better. For optimal health, human beings are wise to adopt an anymal who needs a home, and to gently share company with anymals, and not to eat anymal products.

Heart Disease

In wealthier nations, the biggest killer (by far) is heart disease and coronary artery bypass surgeries are "the most commonly performed cardiac surgery procedure worldwide." [53] These medical problems have been scientifically linked to dietary choices, especially the consumption of saturated fats through choices such as red meats, processed meats, and cheese.[54] (Other key factors are obesity, inactivity, and smoking.). Consuming anymal products introduces LDL cholesterol, which often accumulates so as to ultimately clog the blood's passage. There is no LDL cholesterol in a vegan diet.

Stroke

Strokes are scientifically linked with diet—with the choice to be an omnivore or vegetarian who eats large quantities of cheese and eggs. Eating anymal products lends to elevated LDL cholesterol, which sticks to and narrows blood passageways, raising blood pressure. With the narrowed passageway, blood passage is more easily blocked, preventing the flow of oxygen-rich blood to the brain. Strokes—a blocked blood supply to the brain—are the second largest medical killers worldwide. Because LDL cholesterol comes from anymal products, a vegan diet avoids introducing LDL cholesterol into the bloodstream. (Other key factors are obesity, inactivity, and smoking.)

Cancers

Especially in wealthier nations, cancer is a major killer in human communities. Red and processed meats are medically linked with certain cancers—certain cancers are linked with omnivorous and vegetarian diets. Liver cancer, for example, is linked with the consumption of aflatoxins in dairy products. The consumption of anymal products is also strongly connected with colorectal cancer, and also with pancreatic and prostate cancers. To a lesser degree, stomach cancers are shaped by dietary choice, implicating anymal products.

Respiratory Diseases

Anymal agriculture spews tons of pollutants into the atmosphere, including dust, ammonia, hydrogen sulfide, and smoke, not to mention the burning of fossil fuels and release of methane, significantly reducing air quality.[55] The proliferation of anymal agriculture in the 20th century is a primary cause of increasingly high incidence of respiratory disease worldwide. Shifting to a plant-based diet helps those who suffer from respiratory disease (and takes measures against climate change). The diet each human being chooses either helps alleviate the sufferings of those with impaired respiratory systems, or in choosing to consume anymal products, contributes to respiratory disease and the sufferings of those with impaired lungs.

Figure 4.1

What is the Healthiest Way to Feed a family?

...Which Leading Killers are Caused by Dietary Choice?

Primary Killers (deaths per year)	Meat, Dairy, Eggs	Plant Based Diet
Heart Disease (697,000)	Yes	No
Cancer (557,300)	Yes	No
Stroke (162,700)	Yes	No
Respiratory Disease (124,800)	No...yes*	No
Diabetes (74,000)	Yes	No
Obesity	Yes	No

(ciker.com)

*Thanks to animalag's mighty contribution to air pollution, respiratory diseases are also linked (indirectly) to diet.

(Image courtesy of Lisa Kemmerer, Ph.D., *Eating Earth*)

Mercury Poisoning

Fish flesh is touted as "healthy meat" in comparison with the flesh of terrestrial anymals. Omega-3 fatty acids found in fishes are credited with helping everything from heart disease to diabetes, but the flesh of fishes contains deadly mercury (as well as "dioxins . . . and polychlorinated biphenyls"—PCBs).[56] Mercury is among the top ten chemicals that pose a major public health concern, and eating fishes and shellfishes is the primary way that human beings consume mercury.

Industries—especially coal plants—pollute the environment with mercury, which flows into streams and lakes, then into seas. Pollutants such as mercury (as well as uranium, and most famously, DDT) cannot be broken down in the body, and so they build up in body tissues. Longer-living predator fishes such as tuna, marlin, shark, mackerel, and swordfish "can have mercury concentrations that are hundreds or thousands of times, possibly even a million times, greater than concentrations in the water in which they swim."[57]

The type of mercury that fishes carry—methyl mercury—is easily absorbed from the digestive tract, and once in the bloodstream, accumulates in the brain.[58] Mercury poisoning "attacks the nervous system, causing drooling, hair loss, uncontrollable muscle twitching, a lurching gait, and difficulties in talking and thinking."[59] There is no safe mercury level for human beings. Even low doses over an extended period of time "cause serious physical and mental impairment": Mercury is a "potent neurotoxin that will kill you."[60]

Antibiotic Resistance

In the ongoing struggle to keep farmed anymals healthy in unsuitable conditions, and also to enhance the efficiency of converting fodder to flesh, "seventy percent of U.S. antibiotics are fed to animals," including fishes in aquaculture.[61] This is a primary cause of the disconcerting "rise of pathogens that defy antibiotics."[62] And whether fed to land or sea anymals, this abundance of drugs causes antibiotic resistance and also pollutes the waterways. Anymal waste ultimately ends up in the water system. Antibiotics harm aquatic life.[63] For example, while farmed fishes are treated with antibiotics, wild fishes—who swim in the same waters—have no such protection. When farmed fishes share diseases, wild fishes perish.

Bacteria

E. coli, shigella, and other life-threatening bacteria live in the fecal matter of farmed anymals. Waste sometimes contaminates flesh in the process of butchering, or simply because there is always manure on cow's teats and often on chicken's eggs. In some ways more disturbing, when manure is spread over fields—a primary way of dumping some of the overabundance of anymal waste that accumulates on factory farms—these bacteria are introduced to food crops. When manure is dumped on beans or spinach, these pathogens contaminate vegan foods.[64] As long as we have an overabundance of anymals pooping on farms, we can expect anymal waste to be spread on fields, risking the health of all consumers.

Zoomorphic Diseases

Diseases sometimes jump from anymals to humans. These illnesses, called zoomorphic diseases, have generally been introduced through anymal agriculture. Factory farms have brought AIDS, SARS, and swine and bird flu to human communities, killing millions of people. It appears that COVID also came to humanity through anymal exploitation—a virus that has already killed millions of human beings in just a few years.

Summary
Scientists have linked a number of serious and prominent medical problems with omnivory and vegetarian diets rich with dairy or eggs. Science indicates that heart attacks, strokes, cancers, respiratory disease, mercury poisoning, antibiotic resistance, deadly bacteria, and zoomorphic diseases are linked with the consumption of flesh, dairy, and eggs, while a balanced, whole-food vegan diet promotes optimal health.

Studies of meat-eating, vegetarian, and vegan Seventh Day Adventists have shown that a plant-based diet confers substantial health benefits. Other studies, such as the China Project, have demonstrated that a plant-based diet is important in preventing many of the chronic diseases that plague the over-nourished West, such as coronary artery disease, stroke, and many common cancers. (Stephen Kaufman, M.D.)[65]

RESOURCES

For more on diet and health, see:
- Physician's Committee for Responsible Medicine. https://www.pcrm.org/.
- Vegetarian Society. https://www.jvs.org.uk/why-vgetarian/health/.
- Vegan Health. https://veganhealth.org/ (including books). https://veganhealth.org/books-on-nutrition/.
- Vegan dietitian Matt Ruscigno. https://mattruscigno.com/about/.
- Vegan Outreach. https://veganoutreach.org/vegan/.
- Norris, Jack and Virginia Messina. *Vegan for Life*. https://www.hachettego.com/titles/jack-norris/vegan-for-life/9780738285856/.

For more on zoonosis, see:
- The World Health Organization. https://www.who.int/news-room/fact-sheets/detail/zoonoses.

- "Emerging Zoonotic Diseases." https://www.frontiersin.org/articles/10.3389/fvets.2020.5 82743/full#F1.
- Animals Australia. https://www.animalsaustralia.org/features/zoonotic-disease-animal-agriculture-wildlife-pandemics.php.
- Animal Legal Defense Fund. https://aldf.org/issue/covid-19-response/.
- "Eating Animals Causes Pandemics." https://www.eatinganimalscausespandemics.com/.

3. OPPRESSION

Flesh, dairy, and eggs tend to feed comparatively privileged human beings, causing harm both to those who eat these foods and to many other individuals and communities. Meat, dairy, and eggs contribute to world hunger, create miserable jobs for the poor, and (in a variety of ways) foster other injustices, including racism, sexism, ableism, heterosexism, and ageism. Choosing to be an omnivore or a vegetarian is yet another form of oppression and injustice.

World Hunger

The world produces copious quantities of grain, yet human beings die for want of food. How can we make decisions at the grocery store to do our part to share the world's grain supply?

While one hen consumes only a small quantity of food each day (depending on variables such as weather and the hen's type, age, and size), one hen eats about 78 pounds of grain in the course of a full year. There are about 30 billion chickens on the planet, and that adds up to a whopping 2.34 trillion pounds of grain consumed annually by chickens—a very large number, indeed. A typical human being can live quite handily on 400 pounds of grain per year (plus 50 pounds of legumes and beans),[66] in which case the entire human population would consume about 3.2 trillion pounds of grain in one year. Grains inefficiently cycled through the worlds many chickens would feed 8 billion people (roughly the world's human population) for more than 8 months, or about 2/3rds of a year. Of course, humans are not only feeding grains to chickens, but also to turkeys, ducks, pigs, and cattle, all on behalf of omnivores and vegetarians. A lactating dairy cow, for example, eats more than 50 pounds of grain *every day*. Given that a human being living on grains and legumes would consume about 400 pounds of grain per year, a dairy cow eats the same amount of grain in eight days as a single human would need for a full year.

One of the reasons that we can feed more people if we eat grains directly is because calories and nutrients are lost when we cycle food through anymals. For example, less than half of a cow's body is edible. A cow burns up calories and nutrients growing and maintaining horns, hooves, viscera, bones, and hair, none of which humans eat. They also burn up energy and nutrients in moving about, generating heat, digesting foods, and regenerating cells. Most of the calories and nutrients that anymals consume are used in the general process of maintaining a body and in day-to-day living.

> Consuming animal products (rather than eating grains directly) wastes 80–90% of the protein, 90–96% of calories, and 100% of grain's carbohydrates and fiber. (Lisa Kemmerer, Ph.D., Eating Earth: Environmental Ethics and Dietary Choice)[67]

According to the United Nations, more than 800 million human beings currently suffer from chronic undernourishment. Our dietary choices decide whether grains feed people or anymals. When we choose anymal products, we invest in breeding and feeding farmed anymals precious grains, and in the process, we waste calories and nutrients. In a vegan world there would be enough grains to feed everyone.

> If we care about those who are hungry, we
> will maintain a plant-based diet, eating grains
> directly. Our dollars decide what sort of
> industries will flourish. Our dollars decide
> where grains will go. Our dollars decide
> whether or not there will be enough food to go
> around. (Lisa Kemmerer, Ph.D., *Animals and World
> Religions*)[68]

The Labor Force

In *Slaughterhouse*, Gail Eisnitz exposed slaughterhouse jobs in the United States as among the worst possible places of employment: "with nearly thirty-six injuries or illnesses per every one hundred workers, meat packing is the most dangerous industry in the United States."[69] Sadly, it is comparatively common for slaughterhouse laborers to be crushed, burned, stabbed or cut, and to lose fingers or limbs in machinery. Jobs are repetitive and boring, which results in yet more injuries. Eisnitz is not the only investigative journalist to expose slaughterhouse work in the United States as unacceptably dangerous:

> Amputations, fractured fingers, second-degree burns and
> head trauma are just some of the serious injuries suffered by
> US meat plant workers every week, according to data seen
> by the Guardian and the Bureau of Investigative Journalism.
> US meat workers are already three times more likely to
> suffer serious injury than the average American worker, and
> pork and beef workers nearly seven times more likely *to suffer
> repetitive strain injuries.* (Andrew Wasley, Christopher Cook, and
> Natalie Jones in *The Guardian*)[70]

Slaughterhouse work is dangerous and physically exhausting. Employees are awash in blood, immersed in killing and dismembering all day long. And yet these dangerous, ugly jobs pay poorly.[71] Slaughterhouses place "nearly as little value on human life as . . . on animal life."[72]

Human beings have long known that cruelty begets cruelty: Eighteenth century philosopher Immanuel Kant wrote, "He who is cruel to animals becomes hard also in his treatment of men."[73] So, it should not be too surprising that cruelty to anymals sometimes begets cruelty to humans.[74] Indeed, studies have again and again demonstrated that violence toward anymals can result in violence toward human beings. For example, a number of the world's most notorious serial killers started their grizzly careers by torturing and killing anymals. Studies also show that those who work in slaughterhouses become desensitized—and violent—as reflected in unusually high incidences of domestic abuse and assault in communities where slaughterhouses are located. Slaughterhouses tend to bring violence to local communities. If laws took the abuse and killing of anymals seriously, human lives would be saved.

One time I took my knife and sliced off the end of a hog's nose, just like a piece of salami. The hog went crazy for a few seconds. Then it sat there looking kind of stupid. So I took a handful of salt and rubbed it on the wound. Now that hog really went nuts. It was my way of taking out frustration. Another time, there was a live hog in the pit. It hadn't done anything wrong, wasn't even running around. It was just alive. I took a three-foot chunk of pipe and I literally beat that hog to death. It was like I started hitting the hog and I couldn't stop. And when I finally did stop, I'd expended all this energy and frustration, and I'm thinking what in God's sweet name did I do. (Gail Eisnitz, investigative journalist, quoting a man who worked in a slaughterhouse)[75]

Given the risks involved, the nature of the work, and the low pay received (for some, without benefits), it is not surprising that slaughterhouse jobs are generally taken by those who lack other options—those who are marginalized and disempowered. Consumers determine production—which jobs are necessary to produce products. What we eat determines where others work. The dietary choices of consumers determine whether people (especially the underprivileged) will work all day in blood and body parts, killing and dismembering, or will instead pick and process leaves, tubers, legumes, fruits, and grains.

> Slaughterhouses and "meat"-processing facilities [are] suffering and death for animals and exploitation for workers. Fortunately, we can choose not to support this cycle of exploitation and suffering by simply adopting a vegan lifestyle. (Food Empowerment Project)[76]

Injustices of Race, Class, Sex, and Reproduction

A diet of flesh, dairy, and eggs feeds several forms of oppression.

Racism and Classism

Because slaughterhouse work tends to be dangerous, requires killing and dismembering all day long, and is low paying, it is almost always marginalized people who work in slaughterhouses, including undocumented immigrants. These immigrants do not have legal protections guaranteed to citizens, and often work with little or no security or benefits.

> Many [slaughterhouse] employers knowingly hire undocumented workers in an effort to satisfy the extremely high turnover rate of the industry, which often exceeds 100% annually. In some cases, they provide incentives

for current workers to recruit family and friends
and even help new workers to create fake social
security cards. Undocumented workers are
constantly faced with the threat of deportation
– either by their employer or by federal raids.
(Food Empowerment Project)[77]

Moreover, factory farms are invariably located in disempowered communities. In the United States, for example, this means not only poor communities, but often Black, brown, and native communities. Because they carry health threats, reduce air and water quality, and thereby generally reduce the quality of life in the area, anymal agriculture facilities operate in communities where residents have relatively little money or political clout. Toxins introduced into the environment are particularly dangerous for children and the unborn.

When people choose to eat products that create jobs that are dangerous and harmful to individuals and families—jobs that will largely be filled by those who are marginalized—they support and further injustice. When people choose to eat products that support industries that create unhealthy environments—and that almost always operate in poorer communities—they support and further injustice.

Sexism

All farmed anymals suffer, particularly on industrialized farms, but females suffer considerably longer and in ways that entail both physical misery and psychological torment. For this reason, choosing a vegetarian diet (which includes dairy products and eggs) increases anymal suffering, particularly when vegetarians increase their dairy and egg consumption to replace meat products.

Hens are manipulated (both genetically and environmentally) to lay 30 times the number of eggs they would lay in their natural environment, which causes all sorts of medical miseries (that are not treated by veterinarians for economic reasons), leading to suffering and drawn-out deaths. From just before sexual maturity and for the rest of their lives, hens are crowded into tiny battery cages that thwart their natural behaviors and instincts. They are never allowed to hatch an egg or mother a chick.[78] Consumers who choose omnivorous or vegetarian diets create the need that maintains this cruel system.

Cows trapped in the dairy industry are repeatedly impregnated so that their lives on dairy farms are an endless cycle of forced pregnancies, birth, loss of young, and intense milking. Cows in the dairy industry frequently suffer from painful udder infections (which is why a certain level of puss is legally acceptable and expected in milk and milk products). Their newborns are usually taken from them immediately so that consumers can drink the mother's milk. Though they struggle mightily to protect their offspring, of course they cannot; they bawl pitifully for days after their young have been taken. Their little ones are sold into the veal industry, which is also among the cruelest of anymal industries and includes every imaginable form of extreme deprivation—loss of mother and mothering, loss of nursing milk, isolation in tight confinement, and loss of life while still a calf.[79] Consumers who purchase ice-cream, cheese, sour cream, yogurt, whipped cream, butter, or any other dairy product, create the need that maintains this cruel system.

Similarly, while feral hogs produce roughly 30 offspring, factory farmed sows produce nearly 100 additional piglets in just a few years. At sexual maturity, and for the rest of their lives, sows are repeatedly forcibly impregnated and confined inside metal bars that are scarcely larger than their bodies (gestation and farrowing crates), thwarting pretty much every natural instinct and typical behavior—they cannot even scratch itches. Their young are taken from them while still nursing and slaughtered before they are a year old.

All of this misery is brought to billions of chickens, cows, and pigs because consumers buy eggs poached and scrambled, with bacon and cheese, because people choose to eat vanilla ice-cream, pot roast, cheeseburgers, strawberry yogurt, and peppery sausages. When choosing what to eat, we decide whether or not to support the exploitation of wombs, nursing milk, and reproductive eggs—whether or not we want to prevent the mothering of young, thereby depriving both young and mothers of the connection they need and long for.

Increases in sex trafficking and the frequency of sexual assault indicate disrespect for—and an exploitative attitude toward—women and girls in many societies. This disrespect and exploitation are reflected in and perpetuated by anymal industries—in the routine exploitation of female biology for profit and food pleasures. To maintain integrity and credibility, those who would wish to protect and respect women, children, and the sacred bond of motherhood, must choose vegan.

[We] condemn other mothers to a lifetime
of exploitation and the most unthinkable loss,
all so we can steal their breast milk, their babies'
food, and . . . we steal their babies from them
too. Their babies. Their bodies. Their milk. Not
ours. (Jessica Strathdee writing of what she witnessed
while living and working on a dairy farm)[80]

Valuing Based on Reproduction (Ableism, Trans Aggression, Ageism, Sexism, Homophobia)

Anymal agriculture reflects and perpetuates a conception of animals as units of production and reproduction, valued according to their productive/reproductive capacities. This approach to anymals devalues individuals, and both reflects and perpetuates a more general failure to respect life—including human life. As ecofeminists have argued, oppressions are connected at their root by an overarching mindset, or worldview, that is reflected and expressed in *any* form of denigration, exploitation, marginalization, or oppression.

Sexism, for example, is interconnected with ageism. As females age, whether hens, sows, cows, or human beings, their fertility declines. Inasmuch as females are expected to "produce" for humanity, their value is perceived as diminishing along with their reproductive capacity. Because of this exploitative attitude, where the ability to birth is part (or all) of the value of a female, cows, sows, and hens are shipped to slaughter as soon as their reproductive abilities decline, though they might otherwise live many more years, were they but given the chance. Where value is rooted in fertility, the value of females decreases with age. It is not surprising, then, that older women tend to be marginalized in many Greco-diaspora (Western) nations.

Similarly, valuing individuals based on production/reproduction devalues the elderly (especially women who are beyond their reproductive years) and those labeled as "disabled" (who are likely be viewed as "less productive"). Valuing based on production/reproduction also lends to devaluing women who are child-free, and anyone in same-sex relationships or trans men and women who are traditionally viewed as unlikely to reproduce.

Hierarchy solidifies and institutionalizes power-over, denigration, marginalization, and exploitation—inequality and oppression. In hierarchical communities, those who are oppressed, whether for race, sex, sexuality, or species, are oppressed due to the same overarching mindset of hierarchy, othering, denigration, oppression, and exploitation.

RESOURCES

For more on what is lost in choosing to eat anymal products, see:
- "So You Want to Stop Devouring Ecosystems? Do the Math!" John Haley in *Animals and the Environment: Advocacy, Activism, and the Quest for Common Ground*. Edited by Lisa Kemmerer (Routledge, 2015). pages 151-162
- *Eating Earth* by Lisa Kemmerer (Oxford 2015).

For more on dietary choice and violence, see:

- Eisnitz, Gail, *Slaughterhouse: The Shocking Story of Greed, Neglect, and Inhumane Treatment Inside the U.S. Meat Industry.* New York: Prometheus, 1997.
- Fitzgerald, Amy. *Animal Abuse and Family Violence: Researching the Interrelationships of Abusive Power.* Mellen Press, 2005.
- Fitzgerald. Amy (et al). https://www.uwindsor.ca/aipabuseresearchgroup/304/amy-fitzgerald-criminology. Also see:
  - "Slaughterhouses and Increased Crime Rates" in *Organization and Environment, 22* (158-184) and
  - "Animal Maltreatment in the Context of Intimate Partner Violence" (in *Violence against Women*).
- Marsh, Peter. *The Supremacist Syndrome: How Domination Underpins Slavery, Genocide, the Exploitation of Women, and the Maltreatment of Animals.* NY: Lantern, 2021.

For stories of people who have transitioned to other forms of employment, see:

- https://freefromharm.org/humane-farmer/.

For more on dietary choice and racism, see:

- The Food Empowerment Project. https://foodispower.org/environmental-and-global/environmental-racism/ and various pages at https://foodispower.org/access-health/.
- Kim, Claire Jean. *Dangerous Crossings: Race, Species, and Nature in a Multicultural Age.* Cambridge: Cambridge UP, 2015.
- "Racism." *Brave Birds.* http://www.bravebirds.org/racism.html.
- Ko, Aph and Syl. *Aphro-Ism: Essays on Pop Culture, Feminism, and Black Veganism from Two Sisters.*

- Marsh, Peter. *The Supremacist Syndrome: How Domination Underpins Slavery, Genocide, the Exploitation of Women, and the Maltreatment of Animals.* NY: Lantern. 2021.

For more on dietary choice and sexism, see:

- *Sister Species: Women, Animals, and Social Justice* by Lisa Kemmerer. Urbana-Champaign: U of IL, 2011.
- Fitzgerald Amy (et al). https://www.uwindsor.ca/sociology/fitzgerald. Especially Also see:
- "Animals, Women and Weapons: Blurred Sexual Boundaries in the Discourse of Sport Hunting." *Society & Animals* 12. 237-251.
- "The Compounding Feminization of Animal Cruelty Investigation Work and Its Multispecies Implications." *Gender, Work, and Organizations.* 2018.
- Mothers Against Dairy. https://mothersagainstdairy.org/.
- Feminists for Animal Rights. http://www.farinc.org/far_articles.html.
- Adams, Carol. *The Pornography of Meat.* NY: Continuum, 2003.
- The Milk Future Museum. https://www.milkfuture.com/.

For more on dietary choice and oppressions, see:

- "The Interconnected Nature of Animal and Earth Activism." *American Behavioral Scientist. Special Issue: Environmental and Animal Defense* 63.8, July, 2019. 1061-1079. https://doi.org/10.1177/0002764219830460 or https://www.researchgate.net/publication/331627321_Th e_Interconnected_Nature_of_Anymal_and_Earth_Activis m
- Chapter One and Two of *Oppressive Liberation: Sexism in Animal Activism.* Palgrave Macmillan, 2023.
- Jewish Veg: Jewish Values in Action: Feeding the World's Hungry. https://www.jewishveg.org/hunger.

- Cassidy, Emily, Paul West, James Gerber· and Jonathan Foley. "Redefining Agricultural Yields." *IOPScience*: Environmental Research. Aug. 2013. https://iopscience.iop.org/article/10.1088/1748-9326/8/3/034015.
- A Well-Fed World: Issues: Hunger. https://awellfedworld.org/global-hunger/.
  - Also "research" and then "hunger" https://awellfedworld.org/.
- World Animal Foundation. https://www.worldanimalfoundation.com/advocate/farm-animals/params/post/1280889/veganism-can-end-world-hunger.
- Brave Birds. http://www.bravebirds.org/hunger.html.
- Adams, Carol and Josephine Donovan, Ed. *Animals and Women: Feminist Theoretical Explorations*. Durham: Duke U. Press, 1995.
- Adams, Carol. The Sexual Politics of Meat: A Feminist-Vegetarian Critical Theory. Continuum, 1990.
- Carter, Christopher. *The Spirit of Soul Food: Race, Faith, and Food Justice*. Champaign: U. of Illinois Press, 2021.
- Kim, Claire Jean. *Dangerous Crossings*. Cambridge UP, 2015.
- Taylor, Sunaura. *Beasts of Burden*. The New Press, 2017.
- Ko, Aph and Syl. Aphro-ism: Essays on Pop Culture, Feminism, and Black Veganism from Two Sisters. Lantern, 2017.
- Jones, Pattrice. *The Oxen at the Intersection*. Lantern, 2014.
- Kemmerer, Lisa, Ed. *Sister Species: Women, Animals, and Social Justice*. U of IL, 2011.

4. RELIGION

All the major religions have taught compassionate and humane treatment of animals. (Al-Hafiz Basheer Ahmad Masri, *Animal Welfare in Islam*)[81]

While religions are many and varied, they all teach that life is ultimately about some larger purpose and that whatever lies beyond this world is shaped by our behaviors and individual choices here on earth. Religious ethics teach people how to live in the here and now in light of what lies beyond.

Although many and varied, religious ethics are remarkably consistent both across traditions and across various branches inside each religious tradition. For example, in light of what lies beyond, all religions teach people to live simply, exemplify humility, be compassionate, and to respect and care for the planet—all of life in particular, including anymals and our health. Importantly, religious ethics hold an expectation of attentive loving-kindness and mercy, especially toward those who are disempowered and disenfranchised.

> *If one focuses on foundational religious texts and core teachings from any of the world's major religions, it is much easier to defend anymal liberation than it is to defend anymal exploitation. Moreover, it is easier to champion anymal liberation than to defend other oft - claimed religious ideals, such as human rights or equality between the sexes. This is understandable when we realize that anymals tend to be extremely vulnerable.*
> (Lisa Kemmerer, Ph.D., *Animals and World Religions*)[82]

Indigenous Teachings

Indigenous religions, emerging before recorded history, generally have no founder and no single text and were passed down through oral traditions of storytelling. While Indigenous religions are varied and independent from one another, they tend to share core teachings, such as the assertion of a scared and interconnected universe, including kinship across species.

> *[N]ature, and the supernatural are all bound in a mutual relationship."* (Pradip Prabhu on indigenous religions in India")[83]
>
> *Man is just another animal. The buffalo and the coyote are our brothers; the birds, our cousins. Even the tiniest ant, even a louse, even the smallest flower you can find—they are all relatives.* (Jenny Leading Cloud of the White River Sioux of central North America)[84]

Indigenous myths do not tend to teach of species as separate and distinct from one another. The division between self and the larger world is not generally part of the indigenous worldview.[85] Instead, "humans share an essential identity with other forms of life"[86] and sacred stories tell of animals moving (either in whole or in part) across species. White Buffalo Woman

(Lakota Nation, great plains and prairies of North America) is both human and buffalo; a young Haida (British Columbia, Canada) who loved to swim morphs to become the first beaver.[87] A Cherokee man moves in with bears, learns to live as they live, and grows thick body hair, though he continues to walk upright. In the far north of north America, a Yup'ik boy spends more and more time among the geese, then lifts off and flies away with the geese-people when autumn comes. Another Yup'ik story tells of a female goose who came to live in the human community, staying out late to eat grass in the marshlands, returning home with mud smeared on her face.[88] These sacred stories show "no division between the animal and human spheres; each takes the other's clothing, shifting appearances at will"—birds, fishes, reptiles, and mammals converse with one another, live in extended communities, and move easily across species boundaries.[89] This "interpenetrability" across species,[90] central to indigenous religions across continents, teaches human beings that living beings are part of a single community and though each looks different, we are kin. Under surface appearances, we share all that is most important.

[T]here is no distinction between the sacred and the profane or even between nature and humans. (Pradip Prabhu on indigenous religions in India)[91]

[E]ach species has its own worldview—a particular perception of reality . . .

For the Chewong, there is no "correct" way of perceiving reality; in order to understand a Panamanian night monkey or a blue chin triggerfish, one must endeavor to see the world through [their] eyes. (Lisa Kemmerer, Ph.D., on the Chewong of Malaysia)[92]

In light of interpenetrability and kinship across species, indigenous stories must some way explain why it is considered perfectly normal, moral, and legal for humans to kill and eat anymal kin when the murder of human beings and cannibalism are shunned. Many creation stories of North America, for example, tell of a time when there was no bloodshed,[93] a time when animals lived peacefully with one another. A Hopi myth recalls a time when the Hopi people lived with anymals "as equals among them."[94] Cherokee stories remember a time of universal peace when "humans and animals freely communicated."[95] The Cheyenne recall an original creation in which "people and animals lived in peace [and] neither people nor animals ate flesh."[96] In Navajo stories, there was a time when all creatures "spoke the same language, and they all had the teeth, claws, feet, and wings of insects."[97] Many ancient indigenous teachings tell of an earlier world of inter-species peace, of a time when there was plenty of food and humans "ate only . . . nuts, seeds, roots, and berries."[98] Sacred indigenous stories teach of a distant past free of omnivory (eating both plant and anymal foods), a world recognized as ideal.

People and animals lived in peace. None, neither people nor animals, ate flesh. (Richard Erdoes and Alfonso Ortiz on the Cheyenne of the Great Plains of North America)[99]

Indigenous sacred stories also record how this perfect peace was broken.[100] In the Cherokee tradition, humans became violent and started to greedily kill anymals for fur and food: "It was easy to do at this time, as the animals were completely unprepared to be hunted and they walked up to human beings, trusting them."[101] In response, anymals "became angry"[102] and met in council. Bears committed to open warfare;[103] other anymals inflicted humans with punishments such as nightmares and diseases.[104]

Maori stories (New Zealand) tell of Tane, father and protector of forests, birds, and insects; Tangaroa, father and protector of fishes and reptiles; and Tu, father and protector of human beings.[105] The three protector gods squabbled, then Tu

attacked Tane's children by hanging nooses to trap birds—
"once caught, he defiled them" by cooking and eating them.[106]
Tu then attacked Tangaroa's children, weaving nets and pulling
fishes from the sea. "These too he defiled" by cooking and
eating them.[107] Ever since, the peace and harmony have
remained broken and "the warrior god and his human children
have dominated and eaten the children of [the] gods of earth and
sea."[108] This narrative of the Maori portrays flesh-eating as an
ugly shift from an original world of peace and harmony, caused
by an angry, warlike god who taught his children (human beings)
to be violent and deadly toward other living beings. It conveys
the idea that flesh-eating defiles anymals—children of the
gods—resulting in angry seas and wild storms that threaten and
kill humans. These Maori narratives teach that many of life's
difficulties and tragedies stem from predation.[109]

A Cheyenne story tells of an earlier time when the world was
an interrelated whole, where all beings "lived together as
friends."[110] But being large and powerful, Buffalo People started
to feel superior and believe that they were entitled to kill and eat
human beings. Humans reminded Buffalo that all creatures were
created equal, that one should not eat others—but also noted
that, should one creature reign supreme, it ought to be human
beings. So, they organized a race to determine who would
dominate. Tellingly, humans knew they would lose in any fair
contest, so they elected birds to race on their behalf. Slim
Buffalo Woman lined up next to hummingbird, meadowlark,
hawk, and magpie—four against one, and no human willing to
race. Magpie won by a feather, and "people became more
powerful than the buffalo and all the other animals"—even the
birds who raced (and won) on behalf of human beings.[111]

*We end our prayers with the words mitakuye oyasin—"all
my relations"—and that includes everything that grows,
crawls, runs, creeps, hops, and flies.* (Jenny Leading Cloud
of the White River Sioux of central North America)[112]

Sacred indigenous stories teach of kinship across species and respect for all life. Sacred stories recall an earlier, preferred time of peace and harmony, a time when all beings lived in community, as equals, without predation. Sacred stories also explain how this ideal state of affairs was destroyed and replaced with predation.[113]

Hindu Teachings

Dear Rama, we are indeed your old good friends from long ago, and your companions of ancient days come here to help you. We are your forefathers. We are your ancestors the animals, and you are our child, Man. As for our friendship, why we've known you a long long time, Rama, and the number of those days is lost in Silence.
(*Ramayana*)[114]

Sacred Hindu teachings hold that all living beings stem from the same source: As a goldsmith fashions many ornaments from one lump of gold, so the Great Goldsmith "makes many ornaments" from one "Universal Spirit."[115] Accordingly, the Eternal/God/Brahman dwells in the *atman* (soul) of each creature—we share a sacred "subtle essence" of all life.[116] Sacred texts teach that each being is thereby linked with every other creature and with God, who "resides as their inner soul."[117] Moreover, with God indwelling in each soul, every living being *is* "the One that lies behind all."[118]

We are connected through this shared essence: As a pinch of salt placed in water cannot be seen or touched, but makes freshwater salty, so the subtle essence of life runs through all, though it cannot be perceived or touched.[119] As all rivers join one great sea, which again rises into the atmosphere to become individual drops, so all living beings—whatever form they might take—shape one body through this sacred, shared "subtle essence."[120] With this knowledge, one sees both God/the

Ultimate and self "in the heart of all beings" and God/the heart of all beings in the individual self.[121] Brahman is atman.

[B]y one clod of clay all that is made of clay is known.
(*Chandogya Upanishad*)[122]

Ahimsa is "the first and foremost ethical principle of every Hindu."[123] Often translated as "not to harm," or "nonviolence," *ahimsa* requires that "no pain should be caused" to any living being, that practitioners abstain "from causing hurt or harm"[124] "in thought, word, or deed"[125] to anyone in "the community of all beings."[126] Hindu ethics teach "love for all creation"[127]—that we are to be "loving and kind" toward all sentient beings.[128] To live with a minimum of harm requires a plant-based diet, and refusing flesh is therefore "considered both appropriate conduct and one's *dharma*" (duty).[129] Many Hindus "shun meat."[130]

Just as the tracks of a snake
and the footprints of other animals
are all covered over in the footprints of an elephant,
so in all the world nonviolence [ahimsa]
is proclaimed to be the highest dharma [duty]. (Christopher
Key Chapple, Ph.D.)[131]

Hindu traditions teach that time has no beginning and that reincarnation/transmigration has been in play for unending eons. In this ongoing process of birth and rebirth, after death the *atman* (imperishable soul) lodges (at conception) in a new life that is nonetheless a continuation of previous lives. The new life is endowed with an age-old *atman* that carries an unending stream of previous thoughts and actions that determine the *atman's* new circumstances and the unfolding of this next life.[132]

In the Hindu worldview, each life is merely "an infinitesimal part of a much larger picture that encompasses all of life" across the unfolding of unending cycles of time. Each *atman* has moved from birth to birth, from body to body, across incalculable ages, connecting all living beings. At some point in the *atman's* long journey, each of us has been a pig prepared for slaughter, a deer pursued and shot by a hunter, and a spider crushed by a thoughtless human being. We have each been every other being's mother, son, and best friend. This ongoing process bonds every living being to every other living being and lends to recognizing Self in every living being and every living being in Self—"A rat is a pig is a dog is a boy."[133]

In light of reincarnation, eating anymals is recognized as "eating the flesh of one's own son" or mother or best friend.[134] Indeed, in a nation where both ethics and law disallow murdering human beings and cannibalism, core Hindu ethics teach that "wanton killing of animals is little better than murder, and meat eating is little better than cannibalism."[135] Those who understand the oneness of all that exists, the "wise ones, who regard the life of [anymals] as their own breath," abstain from eating flesh and praise those who abstain from eating flesh.[136]

If there were no meat-eaters, there would be no killers. A meat-eating man is a killer indeed. (Mahabharata)[137]

The act of the butcher begins with the desire of the consumer. (Satguru Sivaya Subramuniyaswami)[138]

[O]ne who kills beings for the sake of food is the lowest sort of person, a maker of great sin. (Christopher Key Chapple, Ph.D.)[139]

Mahatma Gandhi (a devout Hindu) taught that people "have no right to destroy life that we cannot create."[140] He wrote that in killing anymals for food we ultimately "kill ourselves, our body and soul."[141] Raised without the consumption of flesh or eggs, on learning of "the tortures to which cows and buffaloes were subjected by their keepers," Gandhi gave up milk.[142] Later, he added goat's milk to his diet at the insistence of his wife, but this concession troubled him—Gandhi understood that taking nursing milk was *himsa*, harm/violence against gentle mothers and their young.

> *To my mind the life of a lamb is no less precious than that of a human being. I should be unwilling to take the life of a lamb for the sake of the human body. I hold that, the more helpless a creature, the more entitled it is to protection by man from the cruelty of man.* (Mohandas Gandhi)[143]

Hindus have a long history of eschewing flesh at the table, and despite hundreds of years of British rule (followed by decades of influence from the United States), the vast majority of Hindus continue to avoid both flesh and eggs.

Buddhist Teachings

> *As a mother at the risk of her life watches over her own child, her only child, so also let everyone cultivate a boundless (friendly) mind towards all beings. (Sutta-Nipâta I.8.148)*[144]

Buddhism developed on the outskirts of the Hindu world, inheriting a spiritual philosophy that includes oneness, reincarnation, and a core ethic of *ahimsa*. Buddhism spread throughout India and across Asia, where great thinkers expanded on these earlier ideas, enriching the anymal-friendly ethic of the Indian subcontinent.

Ahimsa, "central to the Buddhist tradition" is "one of the few common features across" all schools of Buddhism—"the sine qua non of [an] ethical life."[145] In addition to this moral obligation of non-harm, Buddhist ethics teach that we are to actively prevent and/or alleviate pain and suffering, and that human beings are to overtly work to bring happiness and peace to all beings.[146]

With all am I a friend, comrade to all,
And to all creatures kind and merciful. ("Buddhist Vows")[147]

Importantly, desires and intentions matter in Buddhist ethics, and they effect karma. Karma means "action" and what we desire and what we intend affects and often guides what we do. Desires, intentions, and actions accumulate in the *atman* (soul) across time (as karma), determining transmigration and incarnation.[148] Through thoughts and deeds we create our futures: "certain actions will lead to suffering while others lead to happiness."[149] Buddhist ethics teach that those who cause misery for others "will not find happiness after death":[150] As surely as one who throws dirt into the wind will have dust in their eyes, one who harms anymals will accumulate negative karma that will bring suffering in their atman's future lives.

As with other religions born on the Indian subcontinent, Buddhist texts teach that each living being has "been mother, father, brother, sister, son, or daughter, or some other relative," and that we are therefore each "kin to all wild and domestic animals, birds, and beings."[151] Reincarnation creates an "interconnected web of life," and all of these relationships "must be respected" in the practice of ahimsa.[152]

All beings tremble before danger, all fear death. When a man considers this, he does not kill or cause to kill.

All beings fear before danger, life is dear to all. When a man considers this, he does not kill or cause to kill. (Dhammapada) [153]

Buddhist philosophers expanded on the philosophy of oneness, positing a reality where it is not possible to distinguish or separate what one mistakenly believes to be an independent "self" from what one mistakenly believes to be "other," providing a vision of radical oneness, of radical interidentification. This version indicates not only that we are all "in this together," but that we *are all this*, "rising and falling as one living body."[154]

Zen Buddhist Thich Nhat Hanh teaches of "interbeing," of a radical oneness where there is no "other." We are not separate from anyone or anything—we do not, and cannot, exist independently: "We have to inter-be with every other thing," which lends to empathizing with a hen, for example, or a toad—feeling their fears and hopes "from within their own perspective,[155] thereby fostering compassion and peaceful coexistence.

A human being is an animal, a part of nature. But we single ourselves out from the rest of nature. We classify other animals and living beings as nature, as if we ourselves are not part of it. Then we pose the question, "How should I deal with Nature?" We should deal with nature the way we deal with ourselves. . . ! Harming nature is harming ourselves, and vice versa. (Thich Nhat Hanh)[156]

Building on the idea of the Ultimate in the individual, Chinese Buddhist thinkers developed the concept of "Buddha-Nature," which holds that the Ultimate (spiritual perfection) is inherent and present in each individual *atman*[157]—perfection in the mundane, ultimate salvation in *this* world. As a consequence, all creatures are perfect, each frog and dog and cow is simultaneously spiritual perfection—Buddha, complete with inherent/spiritual value. This understanding elicits respect and care for all living beings.

Everything is Buddha without exception." (*Everything is Buddha*)[158]

Early Buddhist thinkers concluded that there is no independent "self"[159] (*annata*)—"we" are mere name and form, soon to die and be reborn in yet another name and form, and so it goes. Rejection of any individual self helps steer human beings away from arrogance and general human hubris—what matters is not the illusory temporary self, but the bigger picture and the need to shape positive karma (actions).

Buddhist ethics, which guide practitioners in shaping positive futures, rest on five precepts (laws or rules). The first and most fundamental precept is to "refrain from killing living beings."[160] Central to *ahimsa*, a practicing Buddhist "does not kill [or] cause slaughter,"[161] and the earliest Buddhist teachings and texts remind that the Buddha "forbade flesh altogether among his disciples."[162] Where anymals are concerned, Buddhist "should feel toward them as to their own kin, and, looking on all beings as their only child, should refrain from eating meat."[163] Here again, intentions matter: Practitioners are not merely to stop "the killing of living things," but to foster an attitude of caring, goodwill, and lovingkindness.[164] "A vegan lifestyle is not a dogma, it is an essential element of Buddhist compassion."[165]

"All meat-eating in any form or manner and in any circumstance is prohibited, unconditionally and once and for all." (*Lankavatara Sutra*)[166]

The first precept, oneness, reincarnation, and ahimsa all help to shape the Buddhist rejection of flesh. A Tibetan Buddhist story tells of an advanced practitioner, Aryakatayana, who happens into a home while begging for food. Inside the house, the mother holds a small child on her lap while she eats fish curry, pausing only briefly to abuse an unfortunate dog. Through the "power of intuitive knowledge," accumulated from years of Buddhist practice, Aryakatayana sees previous relationships from earlier lives and marvels that in complete ignorance, this villager is

Eating the flesh of her father,
Beating her mother's back,
And nursing her enemy on her lap.[167]

Jain Teachings

[V]egetarian is excellent for man's physical as well as spiritual health, [but] it is not enough. . . . [B]eing 'vegan' is far superior and a much more complete practice of 'Ahinsa'.[2] (Gurudev Chitrabhanuji)[168]

While there are only about five million Jains on the planet (most of whom live in India), the Jain religion is of particular importance where anymal ethics are concerned. For example, in the hands of Gandhi, Jain "ideals of truth and nonviolence were transformed into powerful tools for bringing about social justice,"[169] and Jains have "contributed much to the eventual triumph of vegetarianism" throughout India.[170]

Jains share core philosophy and ethics with other religions of the Indian subcontinent, including reincarnation, karma (actions determining incarnations), oneness, interconnections, and *ahimsa* (non-harm). The Five Great Vows (*Panch Maha Vrata* or *Mahavrat*) are core to Jain ethics, the first of which is *ahimsa*.

---

[2] *Ahimsa* is sometimes translated into English as "ahinsa."

Ahimsa is a "central ethical principle of Jainism," the importance of which "is difficult to exaggerate":[171] "*Ahimsa paramo dharmah—ahimsa* is the highest duty."[172] Sacred writings remind that "to all beings life is dear" and no being would prefer to be harmed or killed.[173] Ahimsa ought to shape a practitioners thought, intent, word, and deed. Jains must not only abstain from causing harm, but also "wish to harm no living thing," and overtly exhibit "compassion for all living beings."[174]

Jains are expected to (and almost always do) practice *ahimsa* at the table: "Under no circumstances" may any Jain "take meat" or eggs.[175] Omnivory (consuming plants and anymal products) is considered ignorance—"an ignorant man" eats anymal products,[176] and in so doing, harms others and self (through karma):[177] Anymals "all seek happiness" and in hurting anymals we hurt ourselves and "will be born again among them."[178] Many contemporary Jains also eschew dairy, demonstrating that core tenets of the Jain faith can be (and have been) extended to address today's moral concerns—dairy production causes egregious harm and premature death to countless cows and calves.[179]

An infinite number of times have I suffered hopelessly from mallets and knives, forks and maces, which broke my limbs.

Ever so many times have I been slit, cut, mangled, and skinned with keen-edged razors, knives, and shears.

As an antelope I have, against my will, been caught, bound, and fastened in snares and traps, and frequently I have been killed.

As a fish I have, against my will, been caught with hooks and in bow-nets; I have therein been scraped, slit, and killed an infinite number of times.

As a bird I have been caught by [trained] hawks, trapped in nets, and bound with bird-lime, and I have been killed an infinite number of times. . . .

> *Always frightened, trembling, distressed, and suffering, I*
> *have experienced the most exquisite pain and misery. . . .*
> *In every kind of existence I have undergone suffering.*
> (*Uttaradhyayana Sutra*)[180]

Nonharm is essential, but practitioners are also expected to work to alleviate suffering. Toward this end, Jains tend and house stray and injured birds, camels, water buffalo, cows, and so on, at *panjorapors*, which precede contemporary anymal sanctuaries by centuries. *Panjorapors* provide "refuge for injured creatures"[181] where anymals are "cared for, loved, and visited at least once a week by veterinarians."[182]

The third Great Vow, *asteya*, teaches not to take what is not given—not to steal. Of great significance, Jains recognize that this precept applies to human relations with nature and anymals. If we pause to consider what is ours in this vast universe, we are humbled: Neither chickens nor their eggs, cows nor their milk, sows nor their offspring, neither fishes nor shellfishes are ours for the taking. To consume anymals whether hunted, fished, or domesticated, or their nursing milk or eggs, is to take what is not given and break the Jain vow of *asteya*.

> [M]*ilk belongs only to the baby . . . . It is in fact*
> *inhuman and against the principles of non-violence and*
> *non-stealing when humans have milk of cows or other*
> *species, belonging to their offspring.* (Gurudev
> Chitrabhanuji)[183]

Generally expressed in a life of simplicity, the fifth *Mahavrat* is *aparigraha*, or non-possessiveness (non-acquisition, non-grasping, or non-greediness). Practicing *aparigraha* requires examining (and often setting aside) desires, acquiring only what is necessary. Strictly observed by monks and increasingly practiced as householders age, *Aparigraha* prevents acquisitiveness and limits personal possessions, creating a life of simplicity. Through an expectation of simplicity, *Aparigraha* helps to protect the planet and anymals, limiting consumption (which protects habitat) and indicating a vegan diet: Consumers maximize that which they consume and maximize their environmental footprint by eating anymal products, so the fifth *Mahavrat* speaks to a vegan diet.

Confucian and Daoist Teachings

> *Always practice compassion in your heart, commiserating with all. Liberate living beings from captivity and rescue them from danger.* ("The Great Precepts of the Highest Ranks")[184]

Confucian and Daoist teachings are part of one belief system. The teachings of Confucius focus largely on human relationships while Daoism has more of a tendency to explore the larger universe.

Tian (Heaven) is the ultimate religious and moral authority in Confucian writings. The Principle of Heaven, Tianli, is the moral force of the universe—even divine beings are expected to comply with Tianli.[185] The Principle of Heaven "permeates all living things," animals and plants[186] "and is the master of all things."[187] In Confucian writings, the "natural order is a moral order."[188]

The "myriad creatures receive their life" from The Principle of Heaven.[189] Over time, Confucian texts developed the idea of a Great Ultimate, from which all things stem.[190] An original source for all that exists means that all that has come to exist is "organically connected"—"rocks, trees, and animals."[191] Originating a single source establishes "the fundamental similarity of all living things" in an interconnected universe where each living being "forms one body with all things."[192] Confucian texts teach that we are right to recognize all things as our companions on the journey of life.[193]

The humane man regards Heaven and earth and all things as one body. We are not overlords; we are not separate. There is nothing which is not part of [our] self. (Rodney Taylor, Ph.D.)[194]

Importantly, Confucian scholars taught that each living being receives "mind" from the Great Ultimate, and through this endowment of mind from one source, each creature is "simply the one mind of Heaven and Earth."[195] Therefore, there is no fundamental difference in kind between mind in a sheep, human being, dog, or chicken. Confucian texts teach not only that everything is part of a single body but that all that exists is *equal* to self.[196] Shared origins both interconnect and equalize all.

Everything from ruler, minister, husband, wife, and friends to mountains, rivers, spiritual beings, birds, animals, and plants should be truly loved in order to realize my humanity . . . and then my clear character will be completely manifested, and I will form one body with Heaven, Earth, and the myriad things. (Wang Yangming)[197]

Rooted in Tianli, Human beings (*ren*) are understood to be virtuous (*ren*) by nature, so the term *ren* is employed for both. Love is "a defining characteristic" of *ren* (humanity, humaneness, goodness, virtue, benevolence, and love).[198] This attribute is so fundamental to human nature that we are not fully human without *ren*. Confucian writings teach that this is the most important aspect of humanity, "a supreme value more precious than one's own life"— "worth dying for."[199]

Sensitivity to anymals stems naturally from *ren*—given that humans are inherently good, the human mind "cannot bear to see the suffering of others."[200] Confucian writings teach that the moral human being "feels all suffering and every loss of life" as their own personal moral responsibility:[201] "[S]ensitivity to animals is not only ethically suitable but also carries religious authority."[202] Accordingly, Confucius taught his pupils that humans must not take unfair advantage of anymals. Moreover, reflecting Tian and Tianli, human beings ought to be compassionate and express munificent kindness toward anymals.[203]

Where is the limit to our expression of benevolence? (Cheng Yi).[204]

[T]he superior man [is] affected towards animals, [so] that, having seen them alive, he cannot bear to see them die; having heard their dying cries, he cannot bear to eat their flesh. (Mencius)[205]

The Dao (Tao or "Way") shapes the foundation and core of Daoist writings. A concept widely known to be difficult to comprehend, Dao is "the final source and ground of the universe,"[206] ultimate reality,[207] infinite, eternally changeless, nonbeing.[208] Dao runs through the whole universe and is both transcendent and immanent.[209] Permeating all that exists, Dao "abides in all things," shaping and moving every living being.[210] Dao unifies all, providing a measure of perfection (and perfectibility) to all that exists, including each lizard, shrub, and pond.

[Dao is] that reality, or that level of reality, that exists prior to and gave rise to all other things, the physical universe (Heaven and Earth), and all things in it . . . . [The Way] continues in some way to be present in each individual thing as an energy or power, a power that is not static but constantly on the move, inwardly pushing each

thing to develop and grow in a certain way, in a way that is in accord with its true nature. (Robert Henricks, Ph.D.)[211]

[W]hether you point to a little stalk or a great pillar, a leper or the beautiful Hsi-shih,[3] things ribald and shady or things grotesque and strange, the Way [Dao] makes them all into one. (Attributed to Zhuangzi)[212]

Harmony is central to Daoist writings, which describe the cosmos as a place of union, integration, and synthesis. Harmony is a moral ideal, and it is the responsibility of every human being to live "for the fulfillment of the health and harmony of all living things."[213] Daoist writings envision a future time of harmony, a time when various communities of varied species live peacefully on this planet.

Left to their own devises, human beings and animals would form harmonious natural communities. (Attributed to Zhuangzi)[214]

Daoist teachings hold that living beings are neither isolated nor enduring—everything that exists is part of a great and ongoing transformation.[215] After death each body is recycled back into the world of matter and life so that the "chain of being is never broken."[216] Each living being is fundamentally part of this larger whole, part of the unending process of transformation. We die and decompose to become yet other elements in this ever-transforming cosmos.

Endless transformation binds "all things into one, equalizing all."[217] Humans are "one of the myriad kinds of beings"[218]—an intimate part of a larger whole, but of no

---

[3] Legendary woman of great beauty.

greater importance than any other aspect of the universe.[219]
Human beings may tend to envision themselves as
comparatively civilized, educated, and intelligent, but we are
not separate or above other living beings. Humans are animals
among animals, living beings of the earth whose matter, as part
of the universe, has been and will be eternally recycled.

Now a dragon, now a snake,
You transform together with the times,
And never consent to be one thing alone. (Attributed to
Zhuangzi)[220]

Four interlocking ethics stand at the core of Daoism: *ci*
(compassion or deep love), *jian* (restraint or frugality), *bugan wei
tianxia xian* ("not daring to be at the forefront of the world")
and *wuwei* (action as non-action).[221] These four core teachings
shape the moral foundation of Daoist writings, protecting
nature in general and anymals in particular.

Ci, central to Daoist ethics, translates most easily as love,
but "*ci* is deeper, gentler, and broader than love."[222] *Ci* is
manifest as "gentleness, motherly love, commiseration" and
holds the expectation that we foster life.[223] We are to "always
be mindful of the host of living beings,"[224] showing
compassion and empathy "for the sake of all beings."[225]
Human beings are to selflessly "place the myriad beings first"
and not even to "attain the Dao only for" ourselves,[226] but
"help all living beings realize the Dao."[227]

Give wisely to the birds and beasts, to all species of living
creatures. Take from your own mouth to feed them, let
there be none left unloved or not cherished. May they be
full and satisfied generation after generation. May they
always be born in the realm of blessedness.
 Save all that wriggles and runs, all the multitude of
living beings. Allow them all to reach fulfillment and

> *prevent them from suffering and early death. May they all*
> *have lives in prosperity and plenty.* ("The Great Precepts of
> the Highest Ranks")[228]

Jian (restraint, frugality) teaches humans to live simply. In
Daoist teachings, what is natural is ideal, and it is natural for
humans to live simply, like other creatures.[229] Living without
material possessions, anymals exemplify (and teach) *jian*,
revealing that which is truly necessary for existence while
simultaneously exposing that which is superfluous.[230] When
practiced together, *ci* and *jian* encourage human beings to live
simply out of compassion—so that anymals can live without
fear of being consumed or crowded from their homes.

> *The Way of Heaven is to benefit others and not to injure.*
> *(Daode Jing)*[231]

Ci and *jian* are central to *bugan wei tianxia xian* (not daring to
be at the forefront of the world)—humility. Compassion and
simplicity are part of living a humble life, and in Daoist
writings, a humble existence is rightly our path. When humans
place themselves at the forefront, imagining themselves to be
superior or of greater importance, they dominate and exploit
others, including nature and anymals. *Bugan wei tianxia xian*
teaches human beings to take their humble place in the
universe, thereby allowing other creatures to do the same.

An ethic of *wuwei* (nonaction) also encourages human
beings to live "in accordance with nature."[232] *Wu* is "without"
and *wei* translates as "human action intending to achieve
results" that are thought to be "superior to what would result if
nature were simply allowed to take its own course."[233] *Wuwei* is
to behave in such a way as to avoid attempting to control or
change any part of the surrounding world or other creatures in
the hope of improvement, improvement being an assessment
rooted in a myopic human perspective.[234] Manipulating cattle

through breeding plans, debeaking, and artificial insemination are *wei*, manipulations thought by some to be "superior to what would result if nature were simply allowed to take its own course."[235] *Wuwei* carries the expectation that human beings will keep their "hands off the processes at work in the world"[236]—that human beings will not interfere with nature. Nature needs no "improvements" and any such attempts are contrary to Dao and likely to bring undesired results[237]—what is natural is ideal and animals (including human beings) are best left alone.[238]

The world is a spiritual vessel, and one cannot act upon it; one who acts upon it destroys it. (Daode Jing)[239]

What do you mean by Nature and what do you mean by man? . . . .
A horse or a cow has four feet. That is Nature. Put a halter around the horse's head and put a string through the cow's nose, that is man. Therefore it is said, "Do not let man destroy Nature. (Attributed to Zhuangzi)[240]

[A] swamp pheasant . . . doesn't want to be kept in a cage. (Attributed to Zhuangzi)[241]

The primary Daoist precept is not to kill[242] and the "precept to abstain from killing means that you must not kill any living being."[243] Therefore Daoist precepts forbid eating flesh: To eat flesh, even as a guest, is to "violate the precepts."[244]

Do not kill or harm any being. ("The 180 Precepts.")[245]

Daoist precepts often focus on how we treat anymals. Importantly, Daoist precepts warn against causing anymals harm, whether by disrupting their homes, destroying their families, abusing domesticated anymals,[246] or by domestication itself.[247] Domestication, which purposefully manipulates the lives and even the biology of anymals on behalf of profits and/or dietary habits, certainly runs contrary to teachings of *wuwei*.

Jewish Teachings

For more on Judaism and anymals see *Animals and Judaism*: http://lisakemmerer.com/publications.html.

> *As God is merciful, so you also be merciful. As He loves and cares for all His creatures because they are His creatures and His children and are related to Him, because He is their Father, so you also love all His creatures as your brethren. Let their joys be your joys, and their sorrows yours. Love them and with every power which God gives you, work for their welfare and benefit, because they are the children of your God, because they are your brothers and sisters.* (Rabbi Samson Raphael Hirsch, *Horeb* 72:482)[248]

Jewish sacred writings (frequently called scriptures), teach of a single Creator who is sovereign over all that exists and who remains invested in the world. Scriptures teach that, after creating animals, God ordained a plant-based diet (Genesis 1:29)—a world without predation, a world of perfect peace and harmony. Scriptures also indicate that the created universe began and will end with this scriptural ideal—the original peace and harmony of creation will return so that people and anymals once again live together harmoniously, without predation.

> *God said, "See, I have given you every plant yielding seed that is upon the face of all the earth, and every tree with seed in its fruit; you shall have them for food. And to every beast of the earth, and to every bird of the air, and to*

> *everything that creeps on the earth, everything that has the breath of life, I have given every green plant for food." And it was so. God saw everything that he had made, and indeed, it was very good. (Genesis 1:29–31)[249]*

Jewish scriptures teach that human beings are servants of God (Genesis 2:15)—God instructed the first humans to guard and protect creation—"to work, to process, to perform, to labor, to serve (as a servant or slave)"[250] in order to accomplish this task. The language of this passage indicates that our labor on this planet—protecting and tending all of creation on behalf of the Creator—is to be a work of love.[251]

Scriptures teach human beings to be humble; nowhere do scriptures reveal creation as shaped into a hierarchy. Human beings are made along with other land-dwelling animals (6th day); we are all God's creations and are to work together to serve and protect what the Creator has made. Even more explicitly, Jewish sacred writings state that we "are but animals," sharing the same fate—"as one dies, so dies the other" (Ecclesiastes 3:18-19). Jewish sacred writings humble humanity, reminding that we are living creatures among living creatures with "no advantage," that all "have the same breath" and all "go to one place; all are from the dust, and all turn to dust again" (Ecclesiastes 3:19-20.) A human-centered view of scriptures is Aristotelian—not Hebrew—and contradicts what is actually written. God (and God alone) reigns supreme, presiding tenderly over all living beings.

> *The eyes of all look to you,*
> *and you give them their food in due season.*
> *You open your hand,*
> *satisfying the desire of every living thing. (Psalms 145:15)[252]*

The Book of Job teaches humility. When a man named Job indicates that anymals are lower and lesser, the Creator reminds Job that he is their kin—that he is not divine, but rather a living creature among living creatures, created and sustained by God. When Job complains, "I am a brother of jackals, and a companion of ostriches" (Job 30:29), God does not disagree, but replies with a series of telling questions, the first of which is, "Where were you when I laid the foundation of the earth? Tell me, if you have understanding" (Job 38:4). God also recalls the hippopotamus, "which I made just as I made you" (Job 40:15)—a blunt reminder for Job that humans are animals, brought into existence just like other living beings, our companions and kin. Additionally, the Creator reminds Job that creation stands almost exclusively outside of human control and was not made for human beings.[253]

At the close of the story, Job ultimately grasps the lesson, recognizing that he is "brother of jackals, and a companion of ostriches" (Job 30:29), and that God alone is separate and distinct: All beings and all things are God's and we are here to serve the Creator and not ourselves. Human beings are rightly categorized as land animals, as one type of living creature among many types of living creatures. If we view anymals as lowly and lesser, so much the worse for us.

Love, mercy, and compassion are also central to Jewish ethics and written law[254] forbids causing harm to anymals:[255] "It is forbidden, according to the law of the Torah, to inflict pain upon any living creature."[256] Moreover, The Talmud (*Bava Metzia*) conveys a message that human beings are to actively prevent suffering[257]—anymals were created with the expectation that "good should be done to them."[258] Our feelings of compassion should cause the human heartstrings to "vibrate sympathetically with any cry of distress sounding anywhere in creation"[259] and coinciding with these feelings of compassion, "it is our duty to relieve the pain of any creature."[260] God is compassionate, and if we are to do as instructed—to live in the image of God and caretake creation on behalf of the creator, then we must also be compassionate.

He has told you, O mortal, what is good;
and what does the Lord require of you
but to do justice, and to love kindness,
and to walk humbly with your God?
(*Micah* 6:8)[261]

Christian Teachings

For more on Christianity and anymals see *Animals and Christianity:* http://lisakemmerer.com/publications.html.

God's creatures have a derived right to live a natural life and to be loved, cared for, and protected against abuse and exploitation. (Richard Alan Young, Ph.D.)[262]

Core texts of Judaism are also sacred for Christians, providing a moral foundation for a plant-based diet and a life devoted to serving God by caretaking creation. Speaking against human hubris and exceptionalism, these earlier texts teach that all living creatures have personal relations with God and that anymals and humans are kindred through the act of creation—that there is commonality and community across species (rather than hierarchy). Jewish texts also convey the divine expectation that humans not harm anymals and that we actively work to prevent suffering, that we tend to the needs of domesticated anymals so as to keep them contented, satisfied, and at ease.[263] Where ethics are concerned, these earlier texts carry a core message of humility, community across species, service, and kindness and responsibility to anymals as part of service to God in this life.

Christians added to this body of earlier writings with works focused on the life and teachings of Jesus (born into a Jewish community, considered by Christians to be the Christ or anointed son of King David). These authors reveal the significance of Jesus born bodily as a man, and inasmuch as it matters that Jesus was born man for the salvation of humanity, it is no less true or important that Jesus was born human for the salvation of animals (though anymals are generally viewed as blameless and without sin). Human beings are primates, mammals, living creatures of God. Jesus walked the earth in the body of a Mediterranean man, but he died and rose from the dead not just for those who are physically similar, but for all sentient and suffering creation—including anymals:[264] Scriptures teach that all of creation is contained in Christ, all things reconciled through Christ, and that the Creator will ultimately "gather up all things in him, things in heaven and things on earth" (Eph. 1:9–10). "All bodies matter" because God was embodied and then "rose as a body from the grave."[265] Anyone who argues that love is wasted on anymals because Jesus was born a human being may as well argue that love is wasted on women because Jesus was born a man.

For in him all things in heaven and on earth were created . . . all things have been created through him and for him. He himself is before all things, and in him all things hold together. . . . For in him all the fullness of God was pleased to dwell, and through him God was pleased to reconcile all things, whether on earth or in heaven, by making peace through the blood of his cross. (Col. 1:16–20)

In light of the resurrection hope, it is impossible to tolerate animal abuse, exploitation, and oppression. (Richard Alan Young, Ph.D.)[266]

Jesus is the perfect Christian moral exemplar. He exemplified devotion to God through service in this world, living a life of unmitigated humility, love, mercy, and compassion.[267] Jesus did not align with the powerful or the aggressive, but with the marginalized, neglected, and shunned—he is likened to a lamb.

Jesus lived a life that testifies to believing that the world "exists not for the glory of humanity, but for the glory of God" and "since God values and cares for all creation," humans are responsible to tend all that has been created.[268] Toward this end, Jesus was particularly concerned about and sensitive to the needs and sufferings of the downtrodden, demonstrating to humanity that when others stand in great need of help, "the greater is our moral obligation to serve them."[269] Jesus reminds human beings of our duty to serve God by serving those in need, no matter who "they" might be.

> *Jesus did not teach an otherworldly religion; he did not tell his followers to accept the injustices of this world and piously look forward to an afterlife in which goodness and justice would rule. To the contrary, he told his followers that they were to behave in such a way that life on earth would be a reflection of the goodness of the heavenly kingdom. He told them to pray that God's "will be done, on earth as it is in heaven." (Mat. 6:10) (J.R. Hyland)[270]*

Jesus often mentioned The Kingdom of God (or Kingdom of Heaven) in his ministries, referring to the spiritual realm over which God reigns. This kingdom is to be realized and fulfilled here on Earth. Christians, as servants of God, rightly recognize all that exists as God's. Christians owe these vulnerable creatures of God respectful care on behalf of the creator.[271] Anymals are in desperate need of caretaking, particularly anymals exploited for science, clothing, entertainment, flesh, dairy, and eggs.

Jesus demonstrated the expansion of the moral circle, carrying the love of "neighbor" outward to include Samaritans, prostitutes, lepers—whomever was in need; Saint Paul followed his example, extending the circle of love to gentiles (Galatians 3:28). Scriptures hold an expectation that we consciously expand our capacity for and expressions of love, aspiring to unbounded love that reaches not only across nation and race, but across species. If Christians are to serve God by tending creation as the Creator would do, the faithful are obliged to practice munificent love, to dutifully and tenderly care for all that God cares for—all that has been created.

The love of God is all-inclusive and generous; Jesus is often felt by the faithful as munificent love. Scriptures teach that love defines God's nature "in a practical rather than philosophic sense . . . . God's nature is not exhausted by the quality of love, but love governs all its aspects and expressions."[272] Sacred writings indicate that love felt and expressed by human beings originates in the munificence of God's love and connects us back to the Creator.[273] Sacred writings encourage Christ-like love: "True Christian love reflects God's love in showing charity and compassion for all."[274] Love stands at the core of Christian ethics and is "the paramount scripture . . . essential to the Christian way of life."[275]

"Cogito ergo sum: 'I think, therefore I am'? Nonsense. Amo ergo sum: 'I love, therefore I am'" (Sloane Coffin, Ph.D.)[276]

Suffering is central to sacred narratives describing the persecuted Jesus, whose bodily existence culminated in betrayal and death on the cross, often depicted with Jesus wearing a crown of thorns piercing his bleeding forehead. Christian writings teach that Jesus is present in all love and life—and also in all suffering. While God transcends suffering,[277] those who are in pain can "trust that God is with them" and "hold on to God's hand through the suffering."[278] If God is present in the suffering of this world, then God is present in the suffering of anymals.[279] All creatures have eternal significance and whether or not we cause them harm is morally and spiritually important. Whether anymals suffer in laboratories, factory farms, suburban homes, or on fishing lines, when human beings cause suffering, they bring Jesus into that suffering.

> *It is contrary to human dignity to cause animals to suffer or die needlessly.* (The Catechism of the Catholic Church, 2418)[280]

Jesus also exemplifies mercy, another core ethic in Christian writings. All living beings stand in need of mercy and mercy ought to be unbounded, extending to all. Mercy is yet more important for those who are vulnerable, for those who fall under human dominion.[281] The sacred nature of the breath of life, and the complete subjugation of anymals to humanity's ever-growing numbers and power, calls for Christian mercy, for Christ-like tenderness and protection for all living beings.[282] As we require God's mercy, so anymals require our mercy.

> *It is not hard to believe that a merciful God would want His laws to be interpreted in a way that would minimize or eliminate the suffering of animals* (Lewis Regenstein, Ph.D.)[283]
>
> *God loves and cares for creation and has the right to expect this loving care be replicated by humans.* (Richard Alan Young, Ph.D.)[284]

As the quintessential moral exemplar, Jesus called human beings to humble servitude,[285] modeling "compassionate service to others," self-sacrificing service *in this world*.[286] Many known for their proximity to God and for living up to religious ideals—many of those considered saints in the Christian tradition—include anymals in their circle of love and tender care. Sacred stories tell how anymals seek refuge with tenderhearted saints who demonstrate their willingness to serve God by caring for all living creatures. "Indeed, one of the criteria for sainthood seems to be the compassionate treatment of animals."[287]

Islamic Teachings

It is not their eyes that are blind, but their hearts. (Qur'an 22:46)[288]

Islamic writings teach of unity, interconnection, and interdependence: Everything that exists was created by God, who remains a part of everything that has been made.[289] Through God, everything that has been created is "one homogeneous organism" interconnected and interdependent—*all* of creation and the Creator.[290] Sacred Islamic texts teach that the power and splendors of the Creator are revealed everywhere throughout creation—every plant and anymal reminds of the hand of God.[291]

"Islam" means submission—submission to God and "surrender to God's law."[292] The Creator prescribed humans to be servants/vice-regents so that the relationship between humanity and God "is that of slaves to master."[293] Salvation rests on submission to God in this life, in this world. In serving God, the "proper human role is that of conscientious steward"[294]—what is expected is "commensurate humility and sensitivity, predicated upon respect and reverence for the divine purpose in every created thing."[295] As "an instrument of Allah's Will,"[296] we are to serve God by caretaking creation—"humankind has no rights, only duties."[297]

According to the spirit and the overall teachings of Islam, causing avoidable pain and suffering to the defenceless and innocent creatures of God is not justifiable under any circumstances. (Al-Hafiz Basheer Ahmad Masri)[298]

Accounts of the Prophet's life present him as "one of history's most influential social reformers."[299] Sacred writings assure that human beings have a "beautiful model (*uswa hasana*)" in the Prophet,[300] who was compassionate not only toward human beings, but also toward anymals:[301] The Prophet "loved animals and displayed great kindness to them," encouraging others "to do likewise."[302]

He who is devoid of kindness is devoid of good. (Prophet Muhammed)[303]

Human beings are encouraged to live as the Prophet lived, and he extended protective nurturance to anymals. He recognized other living beings as neighbors, as members of their own separate communities—creatures of God who are due human respect and care. In one recollection from the life of Muhammed, the Prophet rebuked a man who wanted to burn a colony of biting ants, referring to the ants as "one of the nations that praise Allah."[304]

[T]he beasts that roam the earth and all the birds that wing their flight are communities like your own. (Qur'an 6:38)[305]

Sacred writings indicate that Muhammed taught and demonstrated "compassion toward animals" as a religious requirement[306]—that killing anymals without justification is "one of the major sins," while acts of kindness and charity to anymals are rewarded. According to the Prophet, a good deed done for an anymal "is as good as doing good to a human being; while an act of cruelty to a beast is as bad as an act of cruelty to a human being."[307] The Prophet reminds that how we treat anymals will matter on the day of judgment,[308] that our interactions with other creatures are of moral and spiritual importance.

[A] true Muslim is one who honors, sustains, and protects the lives of creatures of God. (Richard Foltz, Ph.D.)[309]

A companion of the Prophet is recorded as noting, while crumbling bread for ants, "they are our neighbors and have rights over us."[310] Indeed, anymals even have rights under Islamic law. Islamic law lays out "the right way" for human beings to behave and provides "the ideal social blueprint for a 'good society',"[311] detailing what humans must, may, and may not do in daily life, [312] including what we must, may, and may not do to or with anymals.[313]

Inasmuch as all that exists comes from and remains God's, human vice-regency (assigned by the Creator) requires "due regard for the rights of nature,"[314] and according to Islamic law, human beings are to "respect and pay what is due to each creature," because "each creature has its rights accordingly."[315] According to Islamic law, anymals explicitly have rights over and against human beings,[316] and Islamic law stands as the rightful measure as to what must and may not be done to both free-ranging and domesticated anymals.[317]

According to Islamic law, free-ranging anymals are to remain unfettered:[318] It is forbidden to hold them as "pets." Both trapping and sport hunting are forbidden. Orchestrating anymal fights (whether with free-ranging or domesticated anymals) is also forbidden.[319] According to Islamic law, anymals have a right to remain free and not to be captured, detained, or exploited for human interests.

With regard to domesticated anymals, Islamic law requires those who keep anymals to provide them with clean, ample space—enough space so that they do not harm one another. The basic needs of domesticated anymals are to be satisfied. In fact, they are to be satisfied before human beings tend to their own needs. Humans are forbidden from caging birds. Humans must provide for the retirement of domesticated anymals as they grow old and retirement provisions are to be no less than provisions for younger anymals.

> *No advantages and no urgency of human needs would justify the kind of calculated violence . . . done these days against animals, especially through international trade of livestock and meat.* (Al-Hafiz Basheer Ahmad Masri)[320]

Sacred writings teach that the Creator "desires no injustice to His creatures" (*Qur'an* 3:105–10) and Islamic law is remarkably anymal-friendly,[321] forbidding standard anymal agriculture practices such as crowding and neglect. This puts the force of law behind sacred teachings in any Islamic state.

> *A healthful vegan diet places Muslims on a higher spiritual plane because such a diet reduces pain and suffering, for our bodies and our environment, and allows more people to have access to essential food and water. Choosing a vegan diet is in perfect consonance with Qur'ânic teachings and the Creator's expectations.* (Nadeem Haque on the teachings of his grandfather, Al-Hafiz Basheer Ahmad Masri)[322]

At Cairo's venerable Al-Azhar seminary, jurists (who have tremendous power and authority in the Islamic world) hosted a conference on Islamic law and anymal rights where "scholars of Islamic law, history and philosophy, government officials, veterinarians, and animal rescue workers" concluded that, in light of Islamic law, serious improvements are required in our treatment of anymals, especially anymals exploited for scientific research and food production. This unambiguous conclusion from religious experts, rooted in Islamic law, indicates a vegan diet.

Summary

What [religious person] can reasonably suggest that it is morally or spiritually irrelevant whether or not their purchases cause more or less suffering and premature death? (Lisa Kemmerer, Ph.D., *Animals and World Religions*)[323]

Teachings of the world's largest religions tend to agree that all living creatures, humans and anymals, are fundamentally of the same kind—kindred—and that no species is lesser or spiritually insignificant. The world's largest religions teach that an ideal world is a world without bloodshed and predation. Each major religion puts forward a core ethic of benevolence, kindness, non-harm, love, and compassion; anymals are expected to benefit from these fundamental moral expectations. Human beings are therefore to help anymals who are in need and help alleviate their sufferings, all of which speaks against buying or consuming flesh, dairy, or eggs.

It should not surprise us that the world's dominant religious traditions speak boldly and decisively against selfish, life-destroying exploitation of anymals. In fact, would it not be extremely disappointing to discover, at the end of our extensive study of anymals and world religions, that the egregious suffering and perpetual slaughter of industrial anymal agriculture, the frivolous cruelties of the clothing industry, and the cruel exploitation of anymal experimentation *align* with religious teachings? Would it not be much more troubling to discover that the world's great religions fail to protect anymals from the overwhelming and often unjust power of humanity? (Lisa Kemmerer, Ph.D., *Animals and World Religions*)[324]

For more on animals, ethics, and religions, please see animalsandreligion.org and *Animals and World Religions* at http://lisakemmerer.com/publications.htmlvisit.

RESOURCES

For more on dietary choice and religion, see:

- Tapestry's animalsandreligion.org, which provides extensive information (including books) on religious ethics and anymals. Animalsandreligion.org covers anymals and ethics inside every major religion, including a book for each religion.)
- Also see Kemmerer, *Animals and World Religions.* Oxford UP, 2012.

5. ENVIRONMENT

(Information in this section is indebted to *Eating Earth: Environmental Ethics and Dietary Choice* by Lisa Kemmerer, Ph.D.).

Increasingly, evidence shows that animal agriculture is the primary cause of every major environmental concern, including climate change, deforestation, freshwater reduction, soil degradation, and water pollution. Breeding and keeping large herds and flocks of cattle, goats, sheep, pigs, turkeys, and chickens is extremely damaging to the planet. Anymals are not to blame for this devastation—they are victims. The dietary choices of those who live in industrialized nations are responsible for driving the meat, dairy, egg, and fishing industries that degrade and devastate the environment.

Inefficiency and Waste

Turning anymals into human food is stunningly inefficient: Meat from factory farms has an energy input to output ratio of 35 to one.[325] In this process of waste, stemming largely from feeding grain crops to farmed anymals (who wouldn't exist outside of anymal agriculture industries), rather than eating grains directly, the environment is damaged and sometimes destroyed. While feeding grains to anymals is irrational on several counts, 70% of grains in the United States and 60% of grains in the European Union are grown for and fed to farmed anymals. In the United States, 174 million acres (70 million hectares) of land are devoted to feedcrops, all of which require water and fossil fuels to produce, all of which rob free-ranging anymals of much-needed habitat, including many endangered species.

Grain	Acres/Hectares Planted	Percent of land for Feedcrops	**Acres/Hectares for Feedcrops**
Wheat	54/22 million	20%	11/4.4 million
Soybeans	74/30 million	50%	37/15 million
Corn	74 /30 million	80%	59/24 million
Alfalfa/Hay	67/27 million	100%	67/27 million

Feedcrops in the United States (Image courtesy of Lisa Kemmerer, Ph.D., *Eating Earth*)

Dairy is the worst offender—a lactating cow consumes about 54 pounds of grain every day—enough to supply a typical human being for months.[326] While grains are wasted in cycling them through anymals, millions of people go hungry and are malnourished—in the process, Earth's environments are not only damaged, but sometimes irreparably destroyed.

Feeding hundreds of billions of farmed anymals in order to feed 8 billion people who choose to be omnivores and vegetarians is inefficient. Because so much more grain is required to feed farmed anymals than is necessary to feed human beings directly, a vegan diet requires much less land and many fewer resources. A vegan humanity would need significantly fewer crops and would burn significantly less energy producing food. The most efficient way to feed the world's 8 billion people is with a vegan diet.

Climate Change

Where climate change is concerned, consuming animal products in wealthy nations is fossil fuel intensive, creating ten times more fossil fuel emissions per calorie than plant-based diets.[327] Petroleum is burned to prepare the land, to plant, fertilize, and harvest those millions of tons of feedcrops, which must then be transported and stored. Fossil fuels are also essential for the daily work of factory farms and slaughterhouses, for cleaning, feeding, and transport.[328]

Also important for climate change, anymal agriculture is the largest source of human-induced methane, created and emitted into the environment by the decomposition of manure and the digestion process of the billions of cattle, sheep, and goats bred and raised as "food."[329] Anymal agriculture is also the largest source of human-induced nitrous oxide, which is created and emitted by synthetic fertilizers and the decomposition of manure.[330]

Both methane and nitrous oxide are extremely potent greenhouse gases compared with carbon dioxide: Methane traps solar radiation over 80 times more effectively than carbon dioxide (measured per unit weight) during the 9-15 years it is in the atmosphere; nitrous oxide lingers for about 120 years and traps solar radiation 300 times more effectively than carbon dioxide. To slow climate change, we must reduce anymal agriculture—we must choose vegan.

Freshwater Depletion and Water Pollution

Fresh water is an increasingly pressing environmental concern—we cannot live without clean water. Anymal agriculture is the number one cause of water pollution and freshwater depletion.[331] In the United States, thirteen times more anymal waste than human waste is dumped into water systems—without any treatment.[332] Billions of tons of manure released annually and washed into water systems have caused the exponential growth of dead zones—areas with dead ecosystems.[333] Human-created dead zones did not exist as little as a century ago; now we have roughly 600 dead zones, and the most extensive is larger than the state of Florida or North Korea, considerably larger than Switzerland. The Great Lakes suffer from multiple dead zones and a massive dead zone, caused by agricultural lands along the Mississippi River, has destroyed more than 22,000 km^2/8,500 miles^2 in the Gulf of Mexico.[334]

Species	Tons of poop/year
Chickens (nearly 150,000 Olympic pools)	1 billion
Sheep and goats (nearly 150,000 Olympic pools)	1 billion
Pigs (nearly 150,000 Olympic pools)	1 billion
Cattle (= annual flow of the Hudson River)	1.5 billion

Waste from farmed anymals (Image courtesy of Lisa Kemmerer, Ph.D., *Eating Earth*)

Complicating matters, gigantic herds of farmed anymals (bred and raised for those who consume flesh, dairy, and eggs) drink just under 82 billion liters (22 billion gallons) of water every year.[335] In addition, billions of gallons of water are taken from the world's water systems to grow the billions of tons of crops that are cycled through "livestock." Freshwater is also squandered in other ways, such as hosing down dairies and manure-caked udders before every milking and flushing blood, hair, fat, and bone chips out of slaughterhouses and down the drainpipes.

Species	Average Gallons/liters of Water/Year
Chickens (@ 40 gallons/year/hen)	800 billion/3.6 trillion[4]
Sheep and goats	730 billion/3.3 trillion
pigs	1.825 trillion/8.2 trillion
cattle (@ 7200 gallons/year/bovine)	10.08 trillion/45.8 trillion

Water consumption of farmed anymals (Image courtesy of Lisa Kemmerer, Ph.D., *Eating Earth*)

Habitat Loss and Deforestation

Currently, the biggest threat to endangered species is habitat loss[336] and anymal agriculture is the number one cause of deforestation. Uncultivated lands are usurped both for grazing and for growing yet more feedcrops. In Brazil, creating pasture lands for a lucrative cattle industry is the single largest contributor to the rapid destruction of the Amazon Rainforest.[337] Brazil also exports soy as a feedcrop, supplying

---

[4] Chickens, though small beings, are have a disconcerting environmental impact because humans keep so many chickens and in such large numbers.

nations as far afield as China, Spain, the Netherlands, Thailand, and Iran. Rainforests hold half of Earth's species, foster innumerable medical possibilities, and help to mitigate climate change, yet they are primary targets for creating new grazing and crop lands. These critical and quickly diminishing ecosystems are also home to indigenous communities. We choose against destroying rainforests by choosing vegan.[338]

Would you ever open your refrigerator, pull out 16 plates of pasta, toss 15 in the trash, and then eat just one plate of food? How about leveling 55 square feet of rain forest for a single meal or dumping 2,400 gallons of water down the drain? Of course you wouldn't. But if you're consuming chickens, fish, turkeys, pigs, cows, cow's milk, or eggs, that's what you're doing. (People for the Ethical Treatment of Animals)[339]

Soil Degradation

All but 7% of the earth's soil degradation is caused by anymal agriculture, largely by overgrazing (35%) and deforestation (30%), but also by other agricultural problems, such as intensive production (especially of monocrops raised as feedcrops) and poorly designed irrigation systems. Overgrazing is a well-established norm, and is particularly problematic on public lands, where all citizens bear the cost while only a few profit (those who own ranches and aquaculture facilities).

Unprecedented numbers of cows, sheep, and goats now damage and destroy the surface of the earth, causing erosion, creating dusty wastelands, and turning previously productive land into vast areas that are difficult (if not impossible) to restore.[340] Soil degradation causes food shortages and famine while increasing habitat loss. Soil erosion ultimately creates landscapes that cannot support life, whether free-ranging, domesticated, or human.

Ecosystem and Species Manipulation and Damage

In many nations, the destruction of ecosystems caused by anymal agriculture is made worse by "wildlife control"—government programs that systematically destroy free ranging anymals (grazers and predators) who are considered a threat to the profits of anymal agriculture (including aquaculture) or the success of the human hunt (i.e. a threat to anymals that hunters want as *their* prey). In the United States, for example, more than 50% of the Wildlife Service budget is allocated to killing hundreds of thousands of individuals from such wide-ranging species as prairie dogs, coyotes, foxes, bobcats, and seals. In the process, tens of thousands of other species are killed incidentally.[341] The United States government spends more than $144 million every year managing farmed animals on federal lands—and of this cost, ranchers (those who reap the largest profits) pay only about 20 million.

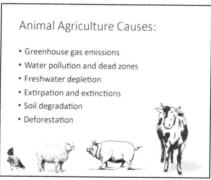

Animal Agriculture Causes:

• Greenhouse gas emissions
• Water pollution and dead zones
• Freshwater depletion
• Extirpation and extinctions
• Soil degradation
• Deforestation

(Image courtesy of Lisa Kemmerer, Ph.D., *Eating Earth*.)[342]

Aquaculture

Earth is also damaged by the cultivation of fishes and other water beings. These facilities destroy habitat wherever they are established. Feed, antibiotics, and high concentrations of waste pollute waters around aquaculture facilities, and when domesticated species escape and mix with wild fishes, aquaculture causes biological contamination. As with land anymals, government wildlife programs kill predators on behalf of the aquaculture industry, including raptors, otters, bears, fishers, and any other free-ranging anymal who discovers the abundant food-supply at an aquaculture facility.

Perhaps most egregiously, farms that raise predatory fishes (like salmon) do not reduce the catch of wild fishes, but only serve to further damage and deplete ecosystems and fishes because they feed wild-caught species to aquaculture fishes. This makes unintended catch—inherent in all forms of fishing—more lucrative, further endangering water populations and water ecosystems.[343] Fishes are individuals (like human beings), and it is rational to assume that they prefer freedom and long life to premature death as part of the pleasures of someone else.) Aquaculture harms and destroys not only farmed fishes, but also free-ranging fishes, usurping habitats, creating pollution, causing biological contamination, bringing predator control that destroys native species, and in the end, resulting in a net loss of life in Earth's water systems.

Industrialized Fishing

Industrialized fishing is also extremely problematic environmentally.[344] About 91 million metric tons of life are pulled from the seas annually by the world's fishing fleet, depleting (and, over time, sometimes destroying) vast water ecosystems. Already, 80% of fisheries have reached or exceeded maximum yields and 90% of large predatory fishes are "fished out"—so greatly diminished that the species is no longer profitable for commercial fisheries. Meanwhile, anymals who depend on sea ecosystems for survival are perishing for want of food, including keystone (and iconic) species such as whales, sealions, and penguins.[345]

Fishing is environmentally disastrous not only because of the sheer numbers of consumers buying fishes and fish products, but also because fishing methods are (universally) indiscriminate, as noted in Chapter One. Lures attract and drown non-target sealife as well as protected sealife as bykill, including birds, marine mammals, and sea turtles. Nets catch and drown dolphins, seals, even whales. Hooks and nets endlessly ensnare billions of beings unintentionally (called bykill or bycatch), including protected and endangered species.[346]

With the introduction of industrial-scale trawling in the Gulf of Thailand, numbers of large sharks, skates, and finfishes declined 60% in just five years.[347] Between 1995 and 2004, numbers of onion-eye grenadiers dropped by more than 93%; roundnose grenadiers dropped "an astonishing 99.6%."[348] (There is no longer any point in fishing commercially for these nearly extinct species, but they continue to be taken as bykill.[349])

Nearly 100% of unintended bykill victims perish—and though devastating for the environment, they can be profitable when sold to aquaculture and other anymal industries as feed. It is yet more difficult to monitor the vast waterways when bykill and illegal fishing prove to be lucrative.

Sea beings killed by ghost nets cannot be sold, and bring no profit, but they (perpetually) add to unintended deaths that stem from fishing. Nets are inevitably lost at sea, becoming "ghost nets" that ensnare and kill sea creatures for as long as their strong nylon fibers last—which is a very long time. Megafleets bearing drift nets "lose an average of six miles of net" every day.[350] At present, more than 10,000 miles (16,000 km) of ghost nets are estimated to be floating the seas.[351] Occasionally online footage is posted of boaters who find ensnared sealife—most often whales—and are able release these huge beings, who are visibly worn out from pulling the heavy fishing nets, from what would otherwise have been a slow death from exhaustion and starvation.

Modern science is as clear as a bell on the terrifying cost of clinging to a non-vegan diet. Whole tracts of virginal land, from the Amazon rainforest to the verdant plains of the Americas, are being plowed over to grow genetically modified soybeans to feed cattle who are injected with poisonous chemicals to cause excessive and rapid growth, merely to provide us with a cheap hamburger. The world's oceans are rapidly becoming devoid of life as overfishing trawls and sucks the last remaining organisms from the depths. . . .

It is up to every single one of us to help make a difference and right these awful wrongs. And it begins at a very simple place . . . on the dinner plate. That is not difficult to accomplish. And that is why I am a vegan. (Lionel Friedberg, author and documentary film director)[352]

Our Taste for Fish

- 80% of fisheries have reached or exceeded maximum yields.
- 90% of large predatory fish (shark, swordfish cod) may already have been removed.
- 91 million metric tons of wildlife are "fished" from the sea annually.

Thanks to fishing, "the world's oceans are in a state of silent collapse" (Pew Oceans Commission)

(Image courtesy of Lisa Kemmerer, Ph.D., *Eating Earth*.)[353]

Hunting and Fishing (as a "sport")

Some people, on learning of the environmental devastation caused by anymal agriculture, decide to hunt and/or fish for at least some of their food. Importantly, these are comparatively expensive ways to put food on the table, due to such costs as gas (to drive to hunting/fishing grounds), licenses, and gear/ammunition. Unlike spending $100 at the grocery store, one might well invest in a hunting/fishing trip and come home emptyhanded. Also of note, a hunter usurps public property, depriving others of the joy of seeing anymals that they have killed and carried home . . . or wounded and left behind.

More importantly, hunting and fishing are extremely damaging to anymals and ecosystems. While killing anymals with modern weapons is not difficult, this does not prevent wounding—lots of wounding. Bird hunting entails a scatter-shot of bullets and has a wounding rate of 30%; bow hunting for deer has a wounding rate of 50%—for every deer killed by a bow hunter, one is left behind to suffer and usually to die a slow death.

Wildlife Control for Hunters and Fishers

There are several other disconcerting environmental problems inherent in the choice to hunt and/or fish. Perhaps most egregiously, governmental programs in many nations manipulate ecosystems on behalf of hunters and fishers, favoring target species and eliminating individuals from competitor species. In the process, hundreds of thousands of anymals who compete with hunter/fisher preferred species (largely predators), are eliminated, including keystone/iconic species such as wolves, bears, and sealions. In the United States, wildlife control eliminates some 2.4 million animals annually, of which more than 120,000 are native carnivores. Of course, non-target species are also killed, particularly by traps, which are as indiscriminate as hooks and nets, catching unintended passers-by, endangered species, and companion animals such as dogs and cats. All of this destruction is paid for by taxpayers, on behalf of hunters/fishers (and ranchers), and costs more than $115 million annually. This despite the fact—because of the fact—that hunters in most nations are a tiny fraction of the overall population, and licenses are unable to fund these expensive and damaging long-term species manipulations. In the United States, only about 5% of the population hunts, and so wildlife management collects a 10% excise tax on handguns (purchased for personal protection and useless for hunting).[354] These environmentally damaging programs that cater to hunters and fishers (and anymal agriculture, including aquaculture) do so at the expense of those who do not feel safe in their inner-city living environments.

Hunters sometimes defend their blood sports as "heritage" or "tradition," hoping to secure their favorite pastime in perpetuity. But as with bride burning, that which is considered "tradition" or "heritage" by powerful, self-interested individuals (who often exploit and harm others in the name of their coveted traditions), is subject to moral scrutiny, and may well be rejected and banned. (Lisa Kemmerer, Ph.D., Eating Earth)[355]

Species Extirpations and Extinctions

Even aside from the devastating effects of government wildlife control programs, hunters, fishers, and anymal agriculture are responsible for species depletions and extinctions, such as the forever-loss of the trusting dodo bird and the gentle Steller's sea cow, and the loss of the beautiful quagga, as well as near-losses (extirpations) of grey wolves and swift foxes—restored at considerable public expense.[356]

Sometimes extinction confronts us in the form of a black and white picture, such as that of Martha, the last passenger pigeon, who died in 1914, alone in a cage in the Cincinnati Zoo. Passenger pigeons were already extinct in the wild, so one single individual—Martha—signaled the loss of a species. Other times, extinction comes in the form of simple nothingness. One day the last individual disappears without humans even knowing what they have caused, or what has been lost. (Kassie Siegel and Brendan Cummings, Center for Biological Diversity's Climate Law Institute, Bear Necessities: Rescue, Rehabilitation, Sanctuary, and Advocacy)[357]

Summary

Changing what we put in our mouth is a simple solution to a handful of the world's most serious ethical problems. Choosing vegan

- is a vote against exploitation, terrible suffering, and premature death for billions of farmed anymals who want to avoid suffering and harms caused by anymal agriculture, and to live.
- helps to protect human beings (especially in wealthier nations) against some of humanity's biggest killers—heart attack, stroke, cancers, and obesity.
- helps to protect marginalized human beings, including the world's hungry and those who work in the anymal industries, as well as those who are likely to be marginalized when production and reproduction determine the value of a life.
- is the most important change we can make to shrink our environmental footprint.[358] Eating anymal products is inefficient and wasteful, and contributes to climate change, freshwater depletion and water pollution, habitat loss and deforestation, soil degradation, and ecosystem and species manipulation and damage.

RESOURCES

For more on dietary choice and environment, see:

- Kemmerer, Lisa. *Eating Earth.* http://lisakemmerer.com/eating_earth.html. Also
- Kemmerer, Lisa. *Animals and Environment.* http://lisakemmerer.com/animals_and_the_environment. html.
- Petter, Olivia. "Veganism is 'Single Biggest Way' to Reduce our Environmental Impact, Study Finds." https://www.independent.co.uk/life-style/health-and-

families/veganism-environmental-impact-planet-reduced-plant-based-diet-humans-study-a8378631.html.

- The Jewish Vegetarian Society. https://www.jvs.org.uk/why-vegetarian/environment/.
- Schwartz, Richard. *Vegan Revolution: Saving Our World, Revitalizing Judaism*. NY: Lantern Publishing & Media, 2020. 45-82.
- Oppenlander, Richard. *Food Choice and Sustainability*. Minneapolis: Langdon Street Press, 2013. Also, Oppenlander, Richard. *Comfortably Unaware: What We Choose to Eat Is Killing Us and Our Planet*. NY: Beaufort Books, 2012.
- A Well-Fed World: Issues: Environment (https://awellfedworld.org/climate/)
- People for the Ethical Treatment of Animals. https://www.peta.org/issues/animals-used-for-food/animals-used-food-factsheets/vegetarianism-environment/.
- Vegan Outreach. https://veganoutreach.org/environment/.
- The Vegan Society. https://www.vegansociety.com/go-vegan/why-go-vegan/environment.
- *Forks Over Knives*. https://www.forksoverknives.com/wellness/vegan-diet-helps-environmental-sustainability/.

For more on diet and waste, see A Well-Fed World
- https://awellfedworld.org/feed-ratios/.

For more on dietary choice, malnutrition, and world hunger, see:
- "Redefining Agricultural Yields." https://iopscience.iop.org/article/10.1088/1748-9326/8/3/034015.
- Jewish Veg. https://www.jewishveg.org/hunger.

- A Well-Fed World. https://awellfedworld.org/, under "research" and then "hunger."
- World Animal Foundation. https://www.worldanimalfoundation.com/advocate/farm -animals/params/post/1280889/veganism-can-end-world-hunger.
- Brave Birds. http://www.bravebirds.org/hunger.html.

CONCLUSION

Choosing to consume flesh, dairy, or eggs (especially in industrialized nations) carries weighty ethical concerns. Changing what we put in our mouth is a vote against exploitation and premature death for farmed anymals, individuals who reason leads us to understand do not want to be exploited or slaughtered (any more than we would want to be) in order to satisfy the taste preferences and eating habits of others. Shifting to a vegan diet helps to protect people (especially in wealthier nations) against some of humanity's biggest killers—heart attack, stroke, cancers, and obesity. Choosing plant-based foods also helps to protect marginalized people, particularly the world's hungry and laborers working in the anymal industries, but also those who are likely to be marginalized when production and reproduction determine the value of a life. Consequently, it is not surprising that a diet protecting anymals, people, and the planet aligns with religious ethics worldwide, which are rooted in compassion and attention to the needs of those who are most vulnerable. Finally, where ethics and diet are concerned, the simple choice to go vegan is the best way to avoid contributing to a host of serious environmental problems, including climate change, freshwater depletion, species loss, water and air pollution (complete with greenhouse gas emissions and dead zones), deforestation, and desertification.

If we have the option to make food choices that protect vulnerable farmed anymals from exploitation and slaughter while also protecting our own health, why not do so? If we have the option to make food choices that help to feed the hungry, and provide jobs that are safer and more desirable to those who are marginalized, why not do so? If we have the option to make food choices that diminish our environmental footprint in a host of critical ways, why would we choose otherwise? When we understand the effects of anymal agriculture, fishing, and hunting, given the weight of ethical concerns involved—harms to anymals, human beings, ecosystems, and the planet—it is easy to see why so many people are now choosing vegan. There is no simpler solution to humanity's most pressing problems.

When you add up the damage that the meat industry does to workers, the environment, and animals, the question [is] "Why wouldn't I go vegan?" (People for the Ethical Treatment of Animals)[359]

While the consumption of flesh, dairy, and eggs (especially in industrialized nations) are encased in a moral quagmire, a diet of grains, legumes, tubers, greens, and fruits (available in most communities and generally much cheaper than anymal products) avoids these disconcerting problems. Where vegan staples such as beans and rice, breads and peanut butter, or potatoes and lentils are available, it is increasingly difficult to understand how any informed individual who sincerely cares about life (whether their own life, the lives of other humans, or the lives of anymals and plants) can neglect to choose vegan. For anymals, people, and the planet, please choose vegan.

RESOURCES

For more on AMORE topics, see:
- YouTube clip, "If Slaughterhouses Had Glass Walls" (https://www.youtube.com/watch?v=p_UpyY2MIOc)
- A Well-Fed World (https://awellfedworld.org/, under the research tab)
- Vegan Outreach (https://veganoutreach.org/why-vegan/)
- The Food Empowerment Project (see "issues" at https://foodispower.org/)
- "Why Vegan?" (short video, which you can find here with a short introduction https://www.youtube.com/watch?v=E7n-Y9UAZtI)

About the Author

Internationally known for working on behalf of anymals, the environment, and disempowered human beings, professor emeritus Dr. Lisa Kemmerer founded and directs the information sharing non-profit, Tapestry. Kemmerer has authored numerous articles and books including *Animals and World Religions*; *Eating Earth: Environmental Ethics and Dietary Choice*, and *Sister Species: Women, Animals, and Social Justice*.

For more information and to support the work of Tapestry, please visit lisakemmerer.com and tapestryofpeace.org.

Endnotes

1 Carter, Christopher. *The Spirit of Soul Food: Race, Faith and Food Justice.*
Urbana: U. of Illinois, 2022. 131.
2 Hussain, Grace. "How Many Animals Are Killed for Food Every Day?"
Sentient Media. Aug. 31, 2022. https://sentientmedia.org/how-many-
animals-are-killed-for-food-every-day/.
3 "Michael Gurwitz" at "Fish Feel: Your Page." *Fish Feel.*
https://fishfeel.org/?s=Gurwitz.
4 Chandroo, Kris, Ian Duncan, and Richard Moccia. "Can Fish Suffer?:
Perspectives On Sentience, Pain, Fear And Stress." *Applied Animal
Behaviour Science* 86.3-4 (2004): 225-250.
https://www.sciencedirect.com/science/article/abs/pii/S016815910400
0498. Also, Bernard Rollin. *Animal Rights and Human Morality.* Amherst,
MA: Prometheus, 1981. 31.
5 Microbiologist Frank Hird in "The Problem with Fishing: Fish and Pain."
PGHMIC: Pittsburgh Independent Media Center. Voices for Animals. July 27,
2005. N.p. http://pittsburgh.indymedia.org/news/2005/07/19545.php.
6 Blankenship, Karl. "Striped Bass Population in Trouble, New Study Finds."
Bay Journal. Feb. 7, 2019. Updated Mar 20, 2020.
https://www.bayjournal.com/news/fisheries/striped-bass-population-in-
trouble-new-study-finds/article_426e274b-3d29-592b-8f81-
85ff7b000dd5.html.
7 "Sports Fishing: Bad for Fish and Other Living Things." *Voices For Animals.*
July 28, 2005. N.p.
http://pittsburgh.indymedia.org/news/2005/07/19545.php.
8 Watson, J. W. and D.W. Kerstetter. "Palegic Longline Fishing Gear: A Brief
History and Review of Search Efforts to Improve Selectivity." *ByCatch
Management Information System.* 40:3 (2006). 6-11. 9. https://www.bmis-
bycatch.org/references/w8xx64tk.
9 Blankenship, Karl. "Scientists Suspect Decline of Herring Is Result of
Bycatch In Other Fisheries." *Chesapeake Bay Journal.* Updated June 2020.
https://www.bayjournal.com/search/?l=25&sort=relevance&f=html&t
=article%2Cvideo%2Cyoutube%2Ccollection&app=editorial&nsa=eedit
ion&q=Scientists+Suspect+Decline+of+Herring+.
10 "Under Pressure, Government Moves to Protect Herring." *In Brief* (Winter
2007-08). 6-7. 7.
11 Guth, Anna. "Court Says Regulators Must Protect Keystone Species from
Giant Trawlers." *EarthJustice.* Feb. 2016. N.p.
https://earthjustice.org/blog/2016-february/court-says-regulators-must-
protect-keystone-species-from-giant-trawlers.
12 Clucas, Ivor. "A Study of the Options for Utilization of Bycatch and
Discards from Marine Capture Fisheries." *FAO Corporate Document
Repository. Fisheries Circular* 928 (1997). Jan. 24, 2009. N.p.
https://www.fao.org/3/w6602e/w6602e00.htm.

[13] *Decline of the Sea Turtles: Causes and Prevention*. National Academies Press. Washington, D.C: National Academy, 1990. 115-16. 24 Jan. 2009. 74-117. 82. https://www.nap.edu/read/1536/chapter/8?term=shrimp#82.

[14] Singer, Peter and James Mason. *The Way We Eat: Why Our Food Choices Matter*. London: Arrow Books. 2006. 126.

[15] Read, Andrew J., Phebe Drinker, and Simon Northridge. "Bycatch of Marine Mammals in U.S. and Global Fisheries." *Conservation Biology* 20: 1 (Feb. 2006). 163–169. 168.

[16] Watson, J. W. and D.W. Kerstetter. "Palegic Longline Fishing Gear: A Brief History and Review of Search Efforts to Improve Selectivity." *ByCatch Management Information System*. 40:3 (2006). 6-11. 9. https://www.bmis-bycatch.org/references/w8xx64tk.

[17] "False Killer Whale *(Pseudorca crassidens)*." *NOAA Fisheries: Office of Protected Resources*. N.p. http://www.nmfs.noaa.gov/pr/species/mammals/cetaceans/falsekillerw hale.htm.

[18] Read, Andrew J., Phebe Drinker, and Simon Northridge. "Bycatch of Marine Mammals in U.S. and Global Fisheries." *Conservation Biology* 20: 1 (Feb. 2006). 163–169. 163.

[19] Readfearn, Graham. "Dolphins Are Still Accidental Casualties of Tuna Fishing." *Science*. N.p. Accessed at *Wired*. https://www.wired.com/story/dolphins-are-still-accidental-casualties-of-tuna-fishing/.

[20] "Vaquita." *NOAA Fisheries: Species Directory*. N.d. https://www.fisheries.noaa.gov/species/vaquita.

[21] Dalton, Rex. "Net Loses Pose Extinction Risk for Porpoise." *Nature* 429.6992 (2004): 590; "The Vanishing Vaquita." *AWI Quarterly* 57:4 (Fall 2008). 21; Rodríguez-Quiroz, Gerardo, Eugenio Alberto Aragón-Noriega, Miguel A. Cisneros-Mata and Alfredo Ortega. "Fisheries and Biodiversity in the Upper Gulf of California, Mexico." *Oceanography*. Ed. Marco Marcelli . NY: *InTech*, 2012. 281-296. 291. http://cdn.intechopen.com/pdfs/33951/InTech-Fisheries_and_biodiversity_in_the_upper_gulf_of_california_mexico.pdf

[22] "Seabirds Needn't Die in Vain." *New Scientist* 195.261 (2007): 6.

[23] Watson, J. W. and D.W. Kerstetter. "Palegic Longline Fishing Gear: A Brief History and Review of Search Efforts to Improve Selectivity." *ByCatch Management Information System*. 40:3 (2006). 6-11. 9. https://www.bmis-bycatch.org/references/w8xx64tk.

[24] Clucas, Ivor. "A Study of the Options for Utilization of Bycatch and Discards from Marine Capture Fisheries." FAO Corporate Document Repository. *Fisheries Circular* 928 (1997). Jan. 24, 2009. N.p. https://www.fao.org/3/w6602e/w6602e00.htm.; "Gulf Sea Turtles Get a Breather: Government Orders Review of Long-Line Fishing." *In Brief* (Summer 2009). 11.

[25] "Gulf Sea Turtles Get a Breather: Government Orders Review of Long-Line Fishing." *In Brief* (Summer 2009). 11.

26 "The State of World Fisheries and Aquaculture in 2020." *Food and Agriculture Organization of the United Nations*. 2020. *https://www.fao.org/state-of-fisheries-aquaculture*. N.p. Accessed at http://www.montereybayaquarium.org/cr/cr_seafoodwatch/issues/.

27 *Fish Feel*. https://fishfeel.org/

28 Jessica Strathdee. *Mothers Against Dairy*. https://mothersagainstdairy.org/dairy-farming-mother/.

29 "Dairy's Dark Side: The Sour Truth behind Milk." *Compassionate Living: The Magazine of Mercy for Animals* 10.6 (Spring–Summer 2010): 10–14. 11.

30 Murray-Ragg, Nadia. "Legal Threshold for Pus Cells in Milk Poised to Rise in Post-Brexit Britain." *LiveKindly: Diet and Nutrition: Food*. N.d. https://www.livekindly.com/legal-threshold-for-pus-cells-in-milk-poised-to-rise-in-post-brexit-britain/.

31 Kevany, Sophie. "More Than 20 Million Farm Animals Die On Way To Abattoir In US Every Year." *The Guardian*. June 15, 2022. https://www.theguardian.com/environment/2022/jun/15/more-than-20-million-farm-animals-die-on-way-to-abattoir-in-us-every-year.

32 Warrick, Jo. "They Die Piece by Piece." *Washington Post*. April 10, 2001. https://www.washingtonpost.com/archive/politics/2001/04/10/they-die-piece-by-piece/f172dd3c-0383-49f8-b6d8-347e04b68da1/.

33 Jacob, Jacqueline P., Henry R. Wilson, Richard D. Miles, Gary D. Butcher, and F. Ben Mather. "Factors Affecting Egg Production in Backyard Chicken Flocks." *IFAS Extension: University of Florida*. May 31, 2018. https://edis.ifas.ufl.edu/publication/PS029.

34 Mormino, Kathy. "Chicken Egg Binding: Causes, Symptoms, Treatment Prevention." *The Chicken Chick*. N.d. https://the-chicken-chick.com/chicken-egg-binding-causes-symptoms/.

35 "Factory Poultry Production." *Farm Sanctuary. FactoryFarming.Com*. http://www.farmsanctuary.org/issues/factoryfarming/poultry/.

36 Kevany, Sophie. "More Than 20 Million Farm Animals Die On Way To Abattoir In US Every Year." *The Guardian*. June 15, 2022. https://www.theguardian.com/environment/2022/jun/15/more-than-20-million-farm-animals-die-on-way-to-abattoir-in-us-every-year.

37 Davis, Karen. "The Social Life of Chickens." *United Poultry Concerns*. Aug. 2008. https://www.upc-online.org/thinking/social_life_of_chickens.html.

38 Kevany, Sophie. "More Than 20 Million Farm Animals Die On Way To Abattoir In US Every Year." *The Guardian*. June 15, 2022. https://www.theguardian.com/environment/2022/jun/15/more-than-20-million-farm-animals-die-on-way-to-abattoir-in-us-every-year.

39 "Pigs." *Animal Liberation Queensland*. https://alq.org.au/pigs.

40 Kemmerer, Lisa. *Eating Earth: Environmental Ethics and Dietary Choice*. Oxford, 2015. 121.

41 Gudorf, Christine E. and James E. Huchingson. *Boundaries: A Casebook in Environmental Ethics*. Washington, DC: Georgetown UP, 2010. 252;

"Reducing Wounding Losses." South Dakota Game, Fish and Parks. http://gfp.sd.gov/hunting/waterfowl/wounding-losses.aspx.

[42] Hatfield, Linda. "Report on Bowhunting." 1. http://animal rightscoalition.com/doc/bowhunting_report.pdf.

[43] Robertson, Jim. *Exposing the Big Game: Living Targets of a Dying Sport.* Winchester, UK: Earth Books, 2012. 134.

[44] Kemmerer, Lisa. *Eating Earth: Environmental Ethics and Dietary Choice.* Oxford: Oxford U. Press, 2014. 30-39.

[45] Luke, Brian. *Brutal: Manhood and the Exploitation of Animals.* Urbana: U. of Illinois P., 2007. 88.

[46] Luke, Brian. *Brutal: Manhood and the Exploitation of Animals.* Urbana: U. of Illinois P., 2007. 88.

[47] "Learn the Facts About Hunting." *The Humane Society of the United States. Washington*, DC: HSUS, 2. n.d.

[48] Robertson, Jim. *Exposing the Big Game: Living Targets of a Dying Sport.* Winchester, UK: Earth Books, 2012. 85.

[49] "Coronary Artery Bypass." *Texas Heart Institute.* https://www.texasheart.org/heart-health/heart-information-center/topics/coronary-artery-bypass/. Also "Coronary artery bypass grafting." *HonorHealth.* https://www.honorhealth.com/medical-services/cardiac-care/treatment-options/coronary-artery-bypass-grafting. And Hargrave, Lauren. "The Costs of Bypass Surgery." March 26, 2019. https://livelyme.com/blog/the-costs-of-bypass-surgery/.

[50] "Understanding Coronary Artery Disease and How to Prevent It." *Healthline.* https://www.healthline.com/health/high-cholesterol/preventing-CAD#lifestyle-adjustments.

[51] "The Top 10 Causes of Death." *World Health Organization.* Dec. 9, 2020. https://www.who.int/news-room/fact-sheets/detail/the-top-10-causes-of-death.

[52] "Having A Dog Can Help Your Heart—Literally." Sept. 1, 2015. *Harvard.edu:* Staying Healthy. https://www.health.harvard.edu/staying-healthy/having-a-dog-can-help-your-heart--literally. Also, see Fields, Lisa. Medically Reviewed by Michael W. Smith, M.D. "6 Ways Pets Can Improve Your Health." Oct. 24, 2013. WebMD. https://www.webmd.com/hypertension-high-blood-pressure/features/6-ways-pets-improve-your-health.

[53] Melly, Ludovic *et al.* "Fifty Years of Coronary Artery Bypass Grafting." *Journal of Thoracic Disease* 10.3 (2018): pp. 1960-1967.

[54] "Foods That Are Bad for Your Heart." *WebMD.* Feb. 10, 2021. https://www.webmd.com/heart-disease/ss/slideshow-foods-bad-heart.

[55] Oppenlander, Richard A. *Comfortably Unaware: Global Depletion and Food Responsibility . . . What You Choose to Eat Is Killing our Planet.* Minneapolis: Langdon Street, 2011. 12.

[56] "Omega-3 Fatty Acids." *University of Maryland Medical Center.* http://www.umm.edu/altmed/articles/omega-3-000316.htm.

[57] Smith, Rick, and Bruce Lourie. *Slow Death by Rubber Duck: The Secret Danger of Everyday Things*. Berkeley: Counterpoint, 2009. 151.

[58] Griesbauer, Laura. "Mercury in the Body and Health Effects." *ProQuest*. Feb. 2007. http://www.csa.com/discoveryguides/mercury/ review4.php.

[59] "Mad as a Hatter." *Corrosion Doctors*. http://corrosion-doctors. org/Elements-Toxic/Mercury-mad-hatter.htm#Erethism.

[60] Smith, Rick and Bruce Lourie. *Slow Death by Rubber Duck: The Secret Danger of Everyday Things*. Berkeley: Counterpoint, 2009. 146.

[61] Kristof, Nicholas. "Our Water-Guzzling Food Factory." *The New York Times*. May 30, 2015. https://www.nytimes.com/2015/05/31/opinion/sunday/nicholas-kristof-our-water-guzzling-food-factory.html.

[62] Kristof, Nicholas. "Our Water-Guzzling Food Factory." *The New York Times*. May 30, 2015. https://www.nytimes.com/2015/05/31/opinion/sunday/nicholas-kristof-our-water-guzzling-food-factory.html.

[63] Hawthorne, Mark. "Planet in Peril." *VegNews* March-Apr. 2012: 34–41. 38.

[64] "E. Coli." *Mayo Clinic*. https://www.mayoclinic.org/diseases-conditions/e-coli/symptoms-causes/syc-20372058.

[65] Kaufman, Stephen. "Harming Animals Harms Humans, part 1: Health. *Christian Vegetarian Association*. https://www.all-creatures.org/articles/an-tpr-reflections-on-lectionary-222.html.

[66] Walker, Mark. "How Much Food Storage For 1 Year." *Build a Stash*. Updated June 10, 2022. https://www.buildastash.com/post/how-much-food-storage-for-1-year

[67] Kemmerer, Lisa. *Eating Earth: Environmental Ethics and Dietary Choice*. Oxford, 2015. 9.

[68] Kemmerer, Lisa. *Animals and World Religions*. Oxford: Oxford UP, 2012. 220.

[69] Eisnitz, Gail. *Slaughterhouse: The Shocking Story of Greed, Neglect, and Inhumane Treatment Inside the U.S. Meat Industry*. New York: Prometheus, 1997. 271.

[70] Wasley, Andrew, Christopher Cook, and Natalie Jones. "Two Amputations a Week: The Cost of Working in a US Meat Plant." *The Guardian*. July 2018. https://www.theguardian.com/environment/2018/jul/05/amputations-serious-injuries-us-meat-industry-plant. Also, see "Slaughterhouse Workers" at the Food Empowerment Project: https://foodispower.org/human-labor-slavery/slaughterhouse-workers/.

[71] Eisnitz, Gail. *Slaughterhouse: The Shocking Story of Greed, Neglect, and Inhumane Treatment Inside the U.S. Meat Industry*. New York: Prometheus, 1997. Also, Newkirk, Ingrid. "Slowing Down Slaughter Speeds is a Step Forward, but we can do far Better." *Daily World*. June 9, 2021. https://www.thedailyworld.com/opinion/commentary-slowing-down-slaughter-speeds-is-a-step-forward-but-we-can-do-far-better/.

[72] Eisnitz, Gail. *Slaughterhouse: The Shocking Story of Greed, Neglect, and Inhumane Treatment Inside the U.S. Meat Industry*. New York: Prometheus, 1997. 273.

[73] Kant, Immanuel. *"Lectures on Ethics."*
http://faculty.smu.edu/jkazez/animal%20rights/IMMANUEL%20KA
NT.htm.

[74] Hoff, Christina. "Kant's Invidious Humanism." *Environmental Ethics* 5
(1983): 63–7 on p. 63–64.

[75] Eisnitz, Gail. *Slaughterhouse: The Shocking Story of Greed, Neglect, and Inhumane
Treatment Inside the U.S. Meat Industry.* New York: Prometheus, 1997.

[76] "Slaughterhouse Workers." *The Food Empowerment Project.*
https://foodispower.org/human-labor-slavery/slaughterhouse-workers/.

[77] "Slaughterhouse Workers." *Food Empowerment Project.*
https://foodispower.org/human-labor-slavery/slaughterhouse-workers/.

[78] Capps, Ashley. "Eggs: What Are You Really Eating?" *Free from Harm.* Feb.
12, 2014. https://freefromharm.org/eggs-what-are-you-really-eating/.

[79] Kemmerer, Lisa. Revised from "Sexism is Speciesism," *Unbounded Project,*
https://unboundproject.org/author/joanne/.

[80] Jessica Strathdee at *Mothers Against Dairy,*
https://mothersagainstdairy.org/dairy-farming-mother/.

[81] Masri, Al-Hafiz Basheer Ahmad. *Animal Welfare in Islam.* Leicestershire:
Islamic Foundation, 2007. 4.

[82] Kemmerer, Lisa. *Animals and World Religions.* Oxford: Oxford UP, 2012.
227.

[83] Prabhu, Pradip. "In the Eye of the Storm: Tribal Peoples of India."
Indigenous Traditions and Ecology: The Interbeing of Cosmology and Community.
Ed. John A. Grim. Cambridge, MA: Harvard U.P. 2001. 47–70. 57.

[84] Erdoes, Richard and Alfonso Ortiz, eds. *American Indian Myths and Legends.*
New York: Pantheon, 1984. 5.

[85] Kwiatkowska-Szatzscheider, Teresa. "From the Mexican Chiapas Crisis: A
Different Perspective for Environmental Ethics." *Environmental Ethics* 19
(1997): 267-78. 276.

[86] Kinsley, David. *Ecology and Religion: Ecological Spirituality in Cross-Cultural
Perspective.* Englewood Cliffs: Prentice-Hall, 1995. 33.

[87] Erdoes, Richard, and Alfonso Ortiz, ed. *American Indian Myths and Legends.*
New York: Pantheon, 1984. 48, 392.

[88] Feinup-Riordan, Ann. "A Guest on the Table: Ecology from the Yup'ik
Eskimo Point of View." *Indigenous Traditions and Ecology: The Interbeing of
Cosmology and Community.* Ed. John A. Grim. Cambridge: Harvard U. 2001.
541-58. 545.

[89] Erdoes, Richard, and Alfonso Ortiz, ed. *American Indian Myths and Legends.*
New York: Pantheon, 1984. 389, 5.

[90] Valladolid, Julio and Frederique Apffel-Marglin. "Andean Cosmovision
and the Nurturing of Biodiversity." *Indigenous Traditions and Ecology: The
Interbeing of Cosmology and Community.* Ed. John A. Grim. Cambridge:
Harvard U. 2001. 639-70. 658.

[91] Prabhu, Pradip. "In the Eye of the Storm: Tribal Peoples of India."
Indigenous Traditions and Ecology: The Interbeing of Cosmology and Community.
Ed. John A. Grim. Cambridge, MA: Harvard U.P. 2001. 47–70. 58.

[92] Kemmerer, Lisa. *Animals and World Religions.* Oxford: Oxford UP, 2012. 38.

[93] Harrod, Howard L. *Renewing the World: Plains Indian Religion and Morality.* Tucson: U Arizona, 1987. 44.

[94] Brown, Dee. *Folktales of the Native American: Retold for our Times.* NY: Henry Holt, 1979. 14.

[95] Bierlein, J.F. *Parallel Myths.* NY: Ballantine, 1994. 115.

[96] Erdoes, Richard, and Alfonso Ortiz, ed. *American Indian Myths and Legends.* New York: Pantheon, 1984. 390.

[97] Rosenberg, Donna. *World Mythology: An Anthology of the Great Myths and Epics.* Lincolnwood: NTC, 1994. 499.

[98] Rosenberg, Donna. *World Mythology: An Anthology of the Great Myths and Epics.* Lincolnwood: NTC, 1994. 499.

[99] Erdoes, Richard, and Alfonso Ortiz, ed. *American Indian Myths and Legends.* New York: Pantheon, 1984. 390.

[100] Harrod, Howard L. *Renewing the World: Plains Indian Religion and Morality.* Tucson: U Arizona, 1987. 44.

[101] Bierlein, J.F. *Parallel Myths.* NY: Ballantine, 1994. 115.

[102] Bierlein, J.F. *Parallel Myths.* NY: Ballantine, 1994. 115.

[103] Spence, Lewis. *North American Indians: Myths and Legends.* London: Studio, 1985. 249.

[104] Bierlein, J.F. *Parallel Myths.* NY: Ballantine, 1994. 115.

[105] Rosenberg, Donna. *World Mythology: An Anthology of the Great Myths and Epics.* Lincolnwood: NTC, 1994. 388.

[106] Rosenberg, Donna. *World Mythology: An Anthology of the Great Myths and Epics.* Lincolnwood: NTC, 1994. 390.

[107] Rosenberg, Donna. *World Mythology: An Anthology of the Great Myths and Epics.* Lincolnwood: NTC, 1994. 390.

[108] Rosenberg, Donna. *World Mythology: An Anthology of the Great Myths and Epics.* Lincolnwood: NTC, 1994. 390.

[109] Rosenberg, Donna. *World Mythology: An Anthology of the Great Myths and Epics.* Lincolnwood: NTC, 1994. 390.

[110] Harrod, Howard L. *Renewing the World: Plains Indian Religion and Morality.* Tucson: U Arizona, 1987. 49.

[111] Erdoes, Richard, and Alfonso Ortiz, ed. *American Indian Myths and Legends.* New York: Pantheon, 1984. 390-92.

[112] Erdoes, Richard and Alfonso Ortiz, eds. *American Indian Myths and Legends.* New York: Pantheon, 1984. 5.

[113] Harrod, Howard L. *Renewing the World: Plains Indian Religion and Morality.* Tucson: U Arizona, 1987. 50.

[114] *Ramayana.* Retold by William Buck. Berkeley: University of California Press, 1976. 315.

[115] Subramuniyaswami, *Satguru Sivaya. Dancing with Siva: Hinduism's Contemporary Catechism.* Concord: Himalayan Academy, 1993. 89.

[116] *Chandogya Upanishad.* Trans. F. Max Muller. *The Upanishads* Part I. New York: Dover, 1962. 1-144. 102.

[117] Dwivedi, O. P. "Dharmic Ecology." *Hinduism and Ecology: The Intersection of*

Earth, Sky, and Water. Ed. Christopher Key Chapple and Mary Evelyn Tucker. Cambridge: Harvard U, 2000. 3-22. 5.

[118] Zaehner, R. C. Hinduism. Oxford: Oxford U, 1962. 7.

[119] *Chandogya Upanishad.* Trans. F. Max Muller. *The Upanishads* Part I. New York: Dover, 1962. 1-144. 92, 104-05.

[120] *Chandogya Upanishad.* Trans. F. Max Muller. *The Upanishads* Part I. New York: Dover, 1962. 1-144. 102.

[121] *Bhagavad Gita.* Trans. Juan Mascaro. Baltimore: Penguin, 1965. 71-72.

[122] *Chandogya Upanishad.* Trans. F. Max Muller. *The Upanishads* Part I. New York: Dover, 1962. 1-144. 92.

[123] Subramuniyaswami, *Satguru Sivaya. Dancing with Siva: Hinduism's Contemporary Catechism.* Concord: Himalayan Academy, 1993. 204.

[124] Subramuniyaswami, *Satguru Sivaya. Dancing with Siva: Hinduism's Contemporary Catechism.* Concord: Himalayan Academy, 1993. 195.

[125] Long, Jeffery D. *Jainism: An Introduction.* NY: I. B. Tauris, 2009. 97.

[126] Kinsley, David. *Ecology and Religion: Ecological Spirituality in Cross-Cultural Perspective.* Englewood Cliffs: Prentice-Hall, 1995. 65.

[127] *Bhagavad Gita.* Trans. Juan Mascaro. Baltimore: Penguin, 1965. 30.

[128] Subramuniyaswami, *Satguru Sivaya. Dancing with Siva: Hinduism's Contemporary Catechism.* Concord: Himalayan Academy, 1993. 181.

[129] Dwivedi, O. P. "Dharmic Ecology." *Hinduism and Ecology: The Intersection of Earth, Sky, and Water.* Ed. Christopher Key Chapple and Mary Evelyn Tucker. Cambridge: Harvard U, 2000. 3-22. 7.

[130] Subramuniyaswami, *Satguru Sivaya. Dancing with Siva: Hinduism's Contemporary Catechism.* Concord: Himalayan Academy, 1993. 205.

[131] Chapple, Christopher Key. "Ahimsa in the Mahabharata: A Story, a Philosophical Perspective, and an Admonishment." *Journal of Vaishnava Studies* 4:3 (Summer 1996): 109–25. 114.

[132] Kinsley, David. *Ecology and Religion: Ecological Spirituality in Cross-Cultural Perspective.* Englewood Cliffs: Prentice-Hall, 1995. 64.

[133] Newkirk, Ingrid. "A Rat Is a Pig Is a Dog Is a Boy." Animals are not Ours. People for the Ethical Treatment of Animals. Aug. 28, 2012., updated 2022. N.p. https://www.peta.org/blog/rat-pig-dog-boy/

[134] Chapple, Christopher Key. "Ahimsa in the *Mahabharata:* A Story, a Philosophical Perspective, and an Admonishment." *Journal of Vaishnava Studies,* 4:3, Summer 1996. 109-125. 114.

[135] Basham, A. L. *The Origins and Development of Classical Hinduism.* Oxford: Oxford U, 1989. 58.

[136] Chapple, Christopher Key. "Ahimsa in the *Mahabharata:* A Story, a Philosophical Perspective, and an Admonishment." *Journal of Vaishnava Studies,* 4:3, Summer 1996. 109-125. 117.

[137] *Mahabharata.* Retold by William Buck. Berkeley: University of California Press, 1973.

[138] Subramuniyaswami, Satguru Sivaya. *Dancing with Siva: Hinduism's Contemporary Catechism.* Concord, CA: Himalayan Academy, 1993. 201.

[139] Chapple, Christopher Key. "Ahimsa in the *Mahabharata:* A Story, a

Philosophical Perspective, and an Admonishment." *Journal of Vaishnava Studies*, 4:3, Summer 1996. 109-125. 120.

140 Gandhi, Mohandas K. *The Essential Gandhi: An Anthology of His Writings on His Life, Work, and Ideas.* Ed. Louis Fischer. NY: Vintage, 2002. 14.

141 Roberts, Holly. *The Vegetarian Philosophy of India: Hindu, Buddhist, and Jain Sacred Teachings.* NY: Anjeli, 2006. 124.

142 Gandhi, Mohandas K. *An Autobiography: The Story of My Experiments with Truth.* Boston: Beacon, 1993. 272–73, 328.

143 Gandhi, Mohandas K. *An Autobiography: The Story of My Experiments with Truth.* Boston: Beacon, 1993. 235.

144 "MettaSutta" and "Uragasutta" (in "Urugavagga"). *The Sutta-Nipâta: The Sacred Books of the East,* Vol. 10. Trans. Fausböll, V. Oxford, UK: Clarendon Press, 1881. 26.

145 Waldau, Paul. *The Specter of Speciesism: Buddhist and Christian Views of Animals.* New York: Oxford, 2002. 143, 138.

146 Hanh, Thich Nhat. *For a Future to be Possible: Buddhist Ethics for everyday Life.* Berkeley: Parallax, 2007. 28.

147 "Buddhist Vows." *The Teachings of the Compassionate Buddha: Early Discourses, the Dhammapada, and Later Basic Writings.* Ed. E. A. Burtt. New York: New American Library, 1955. 79.

148 Conze, Edward, trans. *Buddhist Scriptures.* Bucks: Penguin, 1959. 70-71.

149 Dalai Lama, His Holiness the. *Ethics for the New Millennium.* NY: Riverhead, 1999. 47.

150 *The Dhammapada. The Teachings of the Compassionate Buddha: Early Discourses, the Dhammapada, and Later Basic Writings.* Edt. E. A. Burtt. New York: New American Library, 1955. 59.

151 Chapple, Christopher Key. "Animals and Environment in the Buddhist Birth Stories." *Buddhism and Ecology: The Interconnection of Dharma and Deeds.* Ed. Mary Evelyn Tucker and Duncan Ryuken Williams. Cambridge, Harvard U, 1997. 131-48. 143.

152 Chapple, Christopher Key. "Animals and Environment in the Buddhist Birth Stories." *Buddhism and Ecology: The Interconnection of Dharma and Deeds.* Ed. Mary Evelyn Tucker and Duncan Ryuken Williams. Cambridge, Harvard U, 1997. 131-48. 143.

153 *The Dhammapada: The Path of Perfection.* Trans. Juan Mascaro. New York: Penguin, 1973. 54.

154 Cook, F. H. *Hua-yen Buddhism.* University Park: Penn. State U, 1977. 229.

155 Hanh, Thich Nhat. *Peace is Every Step: The Path of Mindfulness in Everyday Life.* NY: Bantam, 1992. 96, 105.

156 Hanh, Thich Nhat. "The Individual, Society, and Nature." *In The Path of Compassion: Writings on Socially Engaged Buddhism.* Ed. Fred Eppsteiner. Berkeley, CA: Parallax, 1985. 40–46. 41.

157 de Bary, William Theodore, ed. *The Buddhist Tradition in India, China, and Japan.* New York: Vintage, 1972. 156-57, 120.

158 *Everything is Buddha.* Ed. William Theodore de Bary. *The Buddhist Tradition in India, China, and Japan.* New York: Vintage, 1972. 121.

[159] Robinson, Richard H., and Willard L. Johnson. *The Buddhist Religion: A Historical Introduction*. Belmont: Wadsworth, 1997. 38.

[160] Waldau, Paul. *The Specter of Speciesism: Buddhist and Christian Views of Animals*. New York: Oxford, 2002. 136. Also Robinson, Richard H., and Willard L. Johnson. *The Buddhist Religion: A Historical Introduction*. Belmont: Wadsworth, 1997. 77.

[161] Burtt, E. A., ed. *The Teachings of the Compassionate Buddha: Early Discourses, the Dhammapada, and Later Basic Writings*. New York: New American Library, 1955. 71.

[162] de Bary, William Theodore, ed. *The Buddhist Tradition in India, China, and Japan*. New York: Vintage, 1972. 92.

[163] *Lankavatara Sutra. The Buddhist Tradition in India, China, and Japan*. Ed. William Theodore de Bary. New York: Vintage, 1972. 92.

[164] Burtt, E. A., ed. *The Teachings of the Compassionate Buddha: Early Discourses, the Dhammapada, and Later Basic Writings*. New York: New American Library, 1955. 104.

[165] Phelps, Norm. *The Great Compassion: Buddhism and Animal Rights*. New York: Lantern, 2004. 141.

[166] *Lankavatara Sutra. The Buddhist Tradition in India, China, and Japan*. Ed. William Theodore de Bary. New York: Vintage, 1972. 92.

[167] Tashi, Khenpo Phuntsok. "Importance of Life Protection: A Tibetan Buddhist View." Th e Government of Tibet in Exile. http://www.tibet.com/Eco/eco5.html.

[168] Chitrabhanuji, Gurudev. "Ahinsa in Action." "Profiles of Vegan Jains: Gurudev Chitrabhanuji." *Vegan Jains*. Posted June 23, 2013. https://veganjains.com/2013/06/23/profiles-of-vegan-jains-gurudev-chitrabhanuji/

[169] Long, Jeffery D. *Jainism: An Introduction*. NY: I. B. Tauris, 2009. 182.

[170] Jaini, Padmanabh S. *The Jaina Path of Purification*. Dehi: Motilal Banarsidass, 1979. 169.

[171] Long, Jeffery D. *Jainism: An Introduction*. NY: I. B. Tauris, 2009. 99.

[172] Embree, Ainslie T., ed. *Sources of Indian Tradition: From the Beginning to 1800*. New York: Columbia U, 1988. 68.

[173] Embree, Ainslie T., ed. *Sources of Indian Tradition: From the Beginning to 1800*. New York: Columbia U, 1988. 68.

[174] Long, Jeffery D. *Jainism: An Introduction*. NY: I. B. Tauris, 2009. 107, 97, 99.

[175] Jaini, Padmanabh S. *The Jaina Path of Purification*. Dehi: Motilal Banarsidass, 1979. 168.

[176] "Fifth Lecture: Death Against One's Will." Trans. Hermann Jacobi. *Uttarâdhyayana Sutra*. Jaina Sutras, Part II (Sacred Books of the East, Vol. 45). 1895. *Internet Sacred Texts Archive: Jain Texts*. 22 Aug. 2010. http://www.sacred-texts.com/jai/sbe45/sbe4507.htm.

[177] Long, Jeffery D. *Jainism: An Introduction*. NY: I. B. Tauris, 2009. 1.5.5, 107.

[178] *Sutrakrtanga* in *Sources of Indian Tradition: From the Beginning to 1800*. Ed. Ainslie T. Embree. New York: Columbia U, 1988. 63.

[179] Chitrabhanuji, Gurudev. "Ahinsa in Action." "Profiles of Vegan Jains: Gurudev Chitrabhanuji." *Vegan Jains*. Posted June 23, 2013. https://veganjains.com/2013/06/23/profiles-of-vegan-jains-gurudev-chitrabhanuji/

[180] *Uttaradhyayana Sutra* 61-74. "Nineteenth Lecture: The Son of Mriga." Trans. Jacobi, Hermann. *Jaina Sutras, Part II (The Sacred Books of the East, Vol. 45)*. 1895. Verses 63-64. *Internet Sacred Texts Archive*. http://www.sacred-texts.com/jai/sbe45/sbe4521.htm.

[181] Embree, Ainslie T., ed. *Sources of Indian Tradition: From the Beginning to 1800*. New York: Columbia U, 1988. 71.

[182] Tobias, Michael. *Life Force: The World of Jainism*. Berkeley: Asian Humanities Press, 1991. http://www.criticalthink.info/Phil1301/jainism.htm.

[183] Chitrabhanuji, Gurudev. "Ahinsa in Action." "Profiles of Vegan Jains: Gurudev Chitrabhanuji." *Vegan Jains*. Posted June 23, 2013. https://veganjains.com/2013/06/23/profiles-of-vegan-jains-gurudev-chitrabhanuji/

[184] "The Great Precepts of the Highest Ranks." In *Cosmos and Community: The Ethical Dimensions of Daoism*. Livia Kohn. Cambridge: Three Pines, 2004. 175.

[185] Ivanhoe, Philip J., and Bryan W. Van Norden, trans. *Readings in Classical Chinese Philosophy*, 2nd ed. Indianapolis: Hackett, 2001. 50.

[186] Taylor, Rodney L. "Of Animals and Humans." *A Communion of Subjects: Animals in Religion, Science, and Ethics*. Edt. Paul Waldau and Kimberley Patton. New York: Columbia U.P., 2006. 293–307. 293.

[187] Chan Wing-tsit, ed. and trans. *A Source Book in Chinese Philosophy*. Princeton, NJ: Princeton U.P., 1963. 16.

[188] Taylor, Rodney L. "Of Animals and Humans." *A Communion of Subjects: Animals in Religion, Science, and Ethics*. Edt. Paul Waldau and Kimberley Patton. New York: Columbia U.P., 2006. 293–307. 293.

[189] Ivanhoe, Philip J., and Bryan W. Van Norden, trans. *Readings in Classical Chinese Philosophy*, 2nd ed. Indianapolis: Hackett, 2001. 50.

[190] Taylor, Rodney. "Of Animals and Humans." *A Communion of Subjects: Animals in Religion, Science, and Ethics*. Ed. Paul Waldau and Kimberley Patton. New York: Columbia U.P., 2006. 293–307. 300.

[191] Tu, Wei-ming. "The Continuity of Being: Chinese Visions of Nature." *Nature in Asian Traditions of Thought: Essays in Environmental Philosophy*. Ed. J. Baird Callicott and Roger T. Ames. Albany: U of New York, 1989. 67-78. 74-75.

[192] Taylor, Rodney. "Of Animals and Humans." *A Communion of Subjects: Animals in Religion, Science, and Ethics*. Ed. Paul Waldau and Kimberley Patton. New York: Columbia U.P., 2006. 293–307. 293, 301.

[193] Zhang Zai in Taylor, Rodney. "Of Animals and Humans." *A Communion of Subjects: Animals in Religion, Science, and Ethics*. Ed. Paul Waldau and Kimberley Patton. New York: Columbia U.P., 2006. 293–307. 301; also,

Tu Wei-ming. *Confucian Thought: Selfhood as Creative Transformation.* Alabany: State University of NY, 1985. 81, 84.

[194] Taylor, Rodney. "Of Animals and Humans." *A Communion of Subjects: Animals in Religion, Science, and Ethics.* Ed. Paul Waldau and Kimberley Patton. New York: Columbia U.P., 2006. 293–307. 301.

[195] Taylor, Rodney. "Of Animals and Humans." *A Communion of Subjects: Animals in Religion, Science, and Ethics.* Ed. Paul Waldau and Kimberley Patton. New York: Columbia U.P., 2006. 293–307. 301.

[196] Taylor, Rodney. "Of Animals and Humans." *A Communion of Subjects: Animals in Religion, Science, and Ethics.* Ed. Paul Waldau and Kimberley Patton. New York: Columbia U.P., 2006. 293–307. 301.

[197] Yangming, Wang. "Instructions for Practical Living and Other Neo-Confucian Writings." Quoted in Rodney L. Taylor. "Of Animals and Humans." *A Communion of Subjects: Animals in Religion, Science, and Ethics.* Ed. Paul Waldau and Kimberley Patton. New York: Columbia U.P., 2006. 293–307. 302.

[198] Wei-ming, Tu. *Confucian Thought: Selfhood as Creative Transformation.* Alabany: State University of NY, 1985. 81, 84.

[199] Wei-ming, Tu. *Confucian Thought: Selfhood as Creative Transformation.* Alabany: State University of NY, 1985. 88.

[200] Taylor, Rodney. "Of Animals and Humans." *A Communion of Subjects: Animals in Religion, Science, and Ethics.* Ed. Paul Waldau and Kimberley Patton. New York: Columbia U.P., 2006. 293–307. 296, 297.

[201] *Analects of Confucius* in Taylor, Rodney. "Of Animals and Humans." *A Communion of Subjects: Animals in Religion, Science, and Ethics.* Ed. Paul Waldau and Kimberley Patton. New York: Columbia U.P., 2006. 293–307. 306.

[202] Taylor, Rodney. "Of Animals and Humans." *A Communion of Subjects: Animals in Religion, Science, and Ethics.* Ed. Paul Waldau and Kimberley Patton. New York: Columbia U.P., 2006. 293–307. 294.

[203] Taylor, Rodney. "Of Animals and Humans." *A Communion of Subjects: Animals in Religion, Science, and Ethics.* Ed. Paul Waldau and Kimberley Patton. New York: Columbia U.P., 2006. 293–307. 296.

[204] Taylor, Rodney. "Of Animals and Humans." *A Communion of Subjects: Animals in Religion, Science, and Ethics.* Ed. Paul Waldau and Kimberley Patton. New York: Columbia U.P., 2006. 293–307. 301.

[205] Taylor, Rodney. "Of Animals and Humans." *A Communion of Subjects: Animals in Religion, Science, and Ethics.* Ed. Paul Waldau and Kimberley Patton. New York: Columbia U.P., 2006. 293–307. 297.

[206] Xiaogan, Liu. "Non-Action and the Environment Today: A Conceptual and Applied Study of Laozi's Philosophy." *Daoism and Ecology: Ways within a Cosmic Landscape.* Ed. N. J. Girardot et al., Cambridge, MA: Harvard, 2001. 315–40. 322-23.

[207] Henricks, Robert G. *Lao-Tzu Te-Tao Ching: A New Translation Based on the Recently Discovered Ma-wang-tui Texts.* New York: Ballantine, 1989. xviii.

[208] Wu, Yao-Yu. *The Taoist Tradition in Chinese Thought*. Los Angeles: Ethnographics, 1991. 26–27.

[209] Xiaogan, Liu. "Non-Action and the Environment Today: A Conceptual and Applied Study of Laozi's Philosophy." *Daoism and Ecology: Ways within a Cosmic Landscape*. Ed. N. J. Girardot et al., Cambridge, MA: Harvard, 2001. 315–40. 322-23.

[210] Jochim, Christian. *Chinese Religions*. Englewood Cliff s, NJ: Prentice-Hall, 1986. 8. Also Zhuangzi in Wing-tsit Chan, ed. and trans. *A Source Book in Chinese Philosophy*. Princeton, NJ: Princeton U.P., 1963. 203.

[211] Henricks, Robert G. *Lao-Tzu Te-Tao Ching: A New Translation Based on the Recently Discovered Ma-wang-tui Texts*. New York: Ballantine, 1989. xviii–xix.

[212] *Zhuangzi. The Complete Works of Chuang Tzu Translated by Burton Watson*. Trans. Burton Watson. Terebess Asia Online (TAO). http://www.terebess.hu/english/chuangtzu.html.

[213] Kirkland, Russell. "'Responsible Non-Action' in a Natural World: Perspectives from the Neiye, Zhuangzi, and Daode Jing." *Daoism and Ecology: Ways within a Cosmic Landscape*. Ed. N. J. Girardot et al. Cambridge, MA: Harvard U.P., 2001. 283–304. 296.

[214] Zhuangzi. *Wandering on the Way: Early Taoist Tales and Parables of Chuang Tzu*. Ed. Victor Mair. New York: Bantam, 1994. 80.

[215] Thompson, Laurence G. *Chinese Religion: An Introduction*. Belmont: Wadsworth, 1996. 6.

[216] Tu, Wei-ming. "The Continuity of Being: Chinese Visions of Nature." *Nature in Asian Traditions of Thought: Essays in Environmental Philosophy*. Ed. J. Baird Callicott and Roger T. Ames. Albany: U of New York, 1989. 67-78. 70.

[217] Chan Wing-tsit, ed. and trans. *A Source Book in Chinese Philosophy*. Princeton, NJ: Princeton U.P., 1963. 177.

[218] Wu, Yao-Yu. *The Taoist Tradition in Chinese Thought*. Los Angeles: Ethnographics, 1991. 37

[219] Thompson, Laurence G. *Chinese Religion: An Introduction*. Belmont: Wadsworth, 1996. 6.

[220] Zhuangzi in "Human/Nature in Nietzsche and Taoism." Graham Parkes. *Nature in Asian Traditions of Thought: Essays in Environmental Philosophy*. Ed. J. Baird Callicott and Roger T. Ames. Albany: State University of New York Press, 1989. 79–97. 92.

[221] Kirkland, Russell. "'Responsible Non-Action' in a Natural World: Perspectives from the Neiye, Zhuangzi, and Daode Jing." *Daoism and Ecology: Ways within a Cosmic Landscape*. Ed. N. J. Girardot et al. Cambridge, MA: Harvard U.P., 2001. 283–304. 294. Also Liu Xiaogan. "Non-Action and the Environment Today: A Conceptual and Applied Study of Laozi's Philosophy." *Daoism and Ecology: Ways within a Cosmic Landscape*. Ed. N. J. Girardot et al., Cambridge, MA: Harvard, 2001. 315–40. 322-23.

[222] Xiaogan, Liu. "Non-Action and the Environment Today: A Conceptual and Applied Study of Laozi's Philosophy." *Daoism and Ecology: Ways within*

a Cosmic Landscape. Ed. N. J. Girardot et al., Cambridge, MA: Harvard, 2001. 315–40. 330.

223 Xiaogan, Liu. "Non-Action and the Environment Today: A Conceptual and Applied Study of Laozi's Philosophy." *Daoism and Ecology: Ways within a Cosmic Landscape*. Ed. N. J. Girardot et al., Cambridge, MA: Harvard, 2001. 315–40. 330.

224 "The Scripture of the Ten Precepts." In *Cosmos and Community: The Ethical Dimensions of Daoism*. Livia Kohn. Cambridge: Three Pines, 2004. 185.

225 "Record of Purgations of Precepts." In *Cosmos and Community: The Ethical Dimensions of Daoism*. Livia Kohn. Cambridge: Three Pines, 2004. 71, 68.

226 "Great Precepts of Self-Observation." In *Cosmos and Community: The Ethical Dimensions of Daoism*. Livia Kohn. Cambridge: Three Pines, 2004. 215.

227 "The Highest Precepts of Wisdom for the Salvation of All Living Beings." In *Cosmos and Community: The Ethical Dimensions of Daoism*. Livia Kohn. Cambridge: Three Pines, 2004. 168.

228 "The Great Precepts of the Highest Ranks." In *Cosmos and Community: The Ethical Dimensions of Daoism*. Livia Kohn. Cambridge: Three Pines, 2004. *175*.

229 Marshall, Peter. *Nature's Web: Rethinking Our Place on Earth*. London: Cassell, 1992. 19.

230 Anderson, E. N., and Lisa Raphals. "Daoism and Animals." *A Communion of Subjects: Animals in Religion, Science, and Ethics*, Ed. Paul Waldau and Kimberley Patton. New York: Columbia U.P., 2006. 275–90. 278.

231 Chan, Wing-tsit, ed. and trans. *A Source Book in Chinese Philosophy*. Princeton, NJ: Princeton U.P., 1963. 176.

232 Xiaogan, Liu. "Non-Action and the Environment Today: A Conceptual and Applied Study of Laozi's Philosophy." *Daoism and Ecology: Ways within a Cosmic Landscape*. Ed. N. J. Girardot et al., Cambridge, MA: Harvard, 2001. 315–40. 315-16.

233 Kirkland, Russell. "'Responsible Non-Action' in a Natural World: Perspectives from the Neiye, Zhuangzi, and Daode Jing." *Daoism and Ecology: Ways within a Cosmic Landscape*. Ed. N. J. Girardot et al. Cambridge, MA: Harvard U.P., 2001. 283–304. 295.

234 Ip, Po-Keung. "Taoism and the Foundations of Environmental Ethics." *Environmental Ethics* 5 (1983): 335–43. 343.

235 Kirkland, Russell. "'Responsible Non-Action' in a Natural World: Perspectives from the Neiye, Zhuangzi, and Daode Jing." *Daoism and Ecology: Ways within a Cosmic Landscape*. Ed. N. J. Girardot et al. Cambridge, MA: Harvard U.P., 2001. 283–304. 295.

236 *Daode Jing* in Kirkland, Russell. "'Responsible Non-Action' in a Natural World: Perspectives from the Neiye, Zhuangzi, and Daode Jing." *Daoism and Ecology: Ways within a Cosmic Landscape*. Ed. N. J. Girardot et al. Cambridge, MA: Harvard U.P., 2001. 283–304. 296.

237 Kinsley, David. *Ecology and Religion: Ecological Spirituality in Cross-Cultural Perspective*. Englewood Cliffs: Prentice-Hall, 1995. 80.

[238] Anderson, E. N. and Lisa Raphals. "Daoism and Animals." *A Communion of Subjects: Animals in Religion, Science, and Ethics*, Ed. Paul Waldau and Kimberley Patton. New York: Columbia U.P., 2006. 275–90. 297.

[239] *Daode Jing* 29. Kirkland, Russell. "'Responsible Non-Action' in a Natural World: Perspectives from the *Neiye, Zhuangzi*, and *Daode Jing*." In *Daoism and Ecology: Ways within a Cosmic Landscape*. Ed. N. J. Girardot *et al.* Cambridge, MA: Harvard U.P., 2001. 283–304. 296.

[240] *Zhuangzi. A Source Book in Chinese Philosophy*. Ed. and trans. Wing-tsit Chan. Princeton, NJ: Princeton U.P., 1963. 207.

[241] *Zhuangzi. The Complete Works of Chuang Tzu Translated by Burton Watson*. Trans. Burton Watson. Terebess Asia Online (TAO). http://www.terebess.hu/english/chuangtzu.html

[242] Kohn, Livia. *Cosmos and Community: The Ethical Dimensions of Daoism*. Cambridge: Three Pines, 2004. 67.

[243] "Precepts of the Highest Lord Lao." In *Cosmos and Community: The Ethical Dimensions of Daoism*. Livia Kohn. Cambridge: Three Pines, 2004. 148.

[244] "The 180 Precepts." In *Cosmos and Community: The Ethical Dimensions of Daoism*. Livia Kohn. Cambridge: Three Pines, 2004. 144.

[245] "The 180 Precepts." In *Cosmos and Community: The Ethical Dimensions of Daoism*. Livia Kohn. Cambridge: Three Pines, 2004. 138.

[246] Schipper, Kristofer. "Daoist Ecology: The Inner Transformation. A Study of the Precepts of the Early Daoist Ecclesia." *Daoism and Ecology: Ways within a Cosmic Landscape*. Ed. N. J. Girardot et al. Cambridge, MA: Harvard, 2001. 79–94. 84-85.

[247] Kohn, Livia. *Cosmos and Community: The Ethical Dimensions of Daoism*. Cambridge: Three Pines, 2004. 209.

[248] Hirsch, Samson Raphael. *Horeb* 72:482. *Judaism and Vegetarianism*. Richard Schwartz. New York: Lantern, 2001. 24–25.

[249] *Genesis. Holy Bible*. New Revised Standard Version. https://www.bible.com/bible/2016/GEN.1.NRSV

[250] "Biblical Vocabulary: עָבַד ("Serving the Lord")." *Bibleword*. https://www.biblword.net/biblical-vocabulary-serving-the-lord/.

[251] DeWitt, Calvin. "The Three Big Questions." *Worldviews, Religion, and the Environment: A Global Anthology*, Ed. Richard C. Foltz. Belmont: Wadsworth, 2003: 349-355. 353.

[252] *Psalms. Holy Bible*. New Revised Standard Version. https://www.bible.com/bible/2016/GEN.1.NRSV

[253] Vischer, Lukas and Charles Birch. *Living With the Animals*. Geneva: WCC, 1997. 9.

[254] Torah law, particularly Mosaic law in Exodus and Deuteronomy.

[255] "Tza'ar ba'alei Chayim." *Jewish English Lexicon*. https://jel.jewish-languages.org/words/1858.

[256] Ganzfried, Rabbi Solomon. *Code of Jewish Law*, "Book 4, ch 191." NY: Hebrew Publishing Co., 1961. 84. Also, see
- Richard H. Schwartz. *Judaism and Vegetarianism*. NY: Lantern, 2001. 19.

- Dan Cohn-Sherbok. "Hope for the Animal Kingdom." *A Communion of Subjects: Animals in Religion, Science, and Ethics.* Ed. Paul Waldau and Kimberley Patton. NY: Columbia U. Press, 2006. 81-90. 83.
- Medieval commentaries on the Talmud and *Sefer haHinnukh*, thirteenth century "Book of Education."

257 Babylonian Talmud, Bava Metzia 32b. https://www.sefaria.org/Bava_Metzia.32b.11?lang=bi. Also, *Shulchan Aruch (Code of Jewish Law).*

258 Kalechofsky, Roberta. "Hierarchy, Kinship, and Responsibility." *A Communion of Subjects: Animals in Religion, Science, and Ethics.* Ed. Paul Waldau and Kimberley Patton. NY: Columbia U. Press, 2006. 91-99. 95.

259 Rabbi Hirsch's Letter Four of *The Nineteen Letters* in Schwartz, Richard H. *Judaism and Vegetarianism.* NY: Lantern, 2001. 17.

260 Lewis Regenstein in Schwartz, Richard. *Vegan Revolution: Saving Our World, Revitalizing Judaism.* NY: Lantern Publishing & Media, 2021. 146.

261 *Micah. Holy Bible.* New Revised Standard Version. https://www.bible.com/bible/2016/GEN.1.NRSV

262 Young, Richard Alan. *Is God a Vegetarian? Christianity, Vegetarianism, and Animal Rights.* Chicago: Open Court, 1999. 37.

263 Schochet, Elijah Judah. *Animal Life in Jewish Tradition: Attitudes and Relationships.* NY: KTAV Publishing, 1984. 263.

264 Kemmerer, Lisa. *Animals and World Religions.* Oxford: Oxford UP, 2012. 208.

265 Webb, Stephen H. *Good Eating.* Grand Rapids: Brazos, 2001. 162.

266 Young, Richard Alan. *Is God a Vegetarian? Christianity, Vegetarianism, and Animal Rights.* Chicago: Open Court, 1999. 149.

267 Webb, Stephen H. *Good Eating.* Grand Rapids: Brazos, 2001. 145.

268 Young, Richard Alan. *Is God a Vegetarian? Christianity, Vegetarianism, and Animal Rights.* Chicago: Open Court, 1999. 37.

269 Phelps, Norm. *The Dominion of Love.* NY: Lantern, 2002. 150.

270 Hyland, J. R. *God's Covenant with Animals: A Biblical Basis for the Humane Treatment of All Creatures.* New York: Lantern, 2000. 85.

271 Linzey, Andrew. *Animal Theology.* Chicago: U of IL, 1995. 27.

272 Buttrick, George Arthur, ed. and trans. *The Interpreter's Bible* 12 vols. New York: Abingdon, 1956. 12:280.

273 Allen, Clifton J. *Broadman Bible Commentary*, 12 vols. Nashville: Broadman P, 1971. 12:214. Also see "'Dialogue' pg. 164 Chapter on Tears." *Dominican Sisters of Hope: Four Types of Love in the Tradition of Saint Catherine of Siena.* April 29, 2016. https://ophope.org/spirituality/four-types-of-love-in-the-tradition-of-saint-catherine-of-siena/.

274 Young, Richard Alan. *Is God a Vegetarian? Christianity, Vegetarianism, and Animal Rights.* Chicago: Open Court, 1999. 84.

275 Allen, Clifton J. *Broadman Bible Commentary*, 12 vols. Nashville: Broadman, 1971. 12:214.

276 Coffin, Sloane. "The Politics of Compassion: The Heart Is a Little to the Left." *Harvard Divinity Bulletin* 28.2–3 (1999): 11–12. 11.

277 Jenner, Luke. "Does God Suffer with Us? (And How that Question Is Misunderstood)." *Evangelical Times*. April 2014. https://www.evangelical-times.org/articles/biblicaltheological/does-god-suffer-with-us-and-how-that-question-is-misunderstood-1/.

278 "Where is the Pain." https://uscatholic.org/articles/201602/where-there-is-pain-there-is-god/.

279 Linzey, Andrew and Dan Cohn-Sherbok. *After Noah: Animals and the Liberation of Theology*. London: Mowbray, 1997. 129.

280 *Catechism of the Catholic Church* (summary of core Catholic doctrine), Liguori, MO: Liguori, 1994. 2418.

281 Phelps, Norm. *The Dominion of Love*. NY: Lantern, 2002. 154.

282 Polk, Danne W. "Gabriel Marcel's Kinship to Ecophilosophy." *Environmental Ethics* 16 (1994): 173-86. 173 and 185.

283 Regenstein, Lewis in Richard Schwartz. *Vegan Revolution: Saving Our World, Revitalizing Judaism*. NY: Lantern Publishing and Media, 2021. 146.

284 Young, Richard Alan. *Is God a Vegetarian? Christianity, Vegetarianism, and Animal Rights*. Chicago: Open Court, 1999. 149. 37.

285 Webb, Stephen H. *Good Eating*. Grand Rapids: Brazos, 2001. 97.

286 French, William C. "Against Biospherical Egalitarianism." *Environmental Ethics* 17 (1995): 39-57. 488.

287 Webb, Stephen H. *Good Eating*. Grand Rapids: Brazos, 2001.

288 *Qur'an* 22:46. Trans. N. J. Dawood. Harmondsworth, UK: Penguin, 1956.

289 Ozdemir, Ibrahim. "Toward an Understanding of Environmental Ethics from a Qur'anic Perspective." In *Islam and Ecology: A Bestowed Trust*, edited by Richard C. Foltz et al. Cambridge, MA: Harvard U.P., 2003. 3–38. 22.

290 Masri, Al-Hafiz Basheer Ahmad. *Animal Welfare in Islam*. Leicestershire, UK: Islamic Foundation, 2007. 11, 10.

291 Schuon, Frithjof. *Sufism: Veil and Quintessence*. Bloomington, IN: World Wisdom Books, 1979. 21.

292 Esposito, John L. *Islam: The Straight Path*. Oxford: Oxford U.P., 1988. 69.

293 Denny, Frederick M. *Islam and the Muslim Community*. San Francisco: HarperSanFrancisco, 1987. 8.

294 Foltz, Richard C. *Animals in Islamic Tradition and Muslim Cultures*. Oxford, UK: Oneworld, 2005. 15.

295 Said, Abdul Aziz, and Nathan C. Funk. "Peace in Islam: An Ecology of the Spirit." In *Islam and Ecology: A Bestowed Trust*, edited by Richard C. Foltz et al. Cambridge, MA: Harvard U.P., 2003. 155–84. 164.

296 Zaid, Iqtidar H. "On the Ethics of Man's Interaction with the Environment: An Islamic Approach." *Environmental Ethics* 3 (1981): 35–47. 46-47.

297 Denny, Frederick M. *Islam and the Muslim Community*. San Francisco: HarperSanFrancisco, 1987. 8.

298 Masri, Al-Hafiz Basheer Ahmad. *Animal Welfare in Islam*. Leicestershire: Islamic Foundation, 2007. 32, 34.

[299] Berry, Rynn. *Food for the Gods: Vegetarianism and the World's Religions*. New York: Pythagorean, 1998. 244–45.

[300] Foltz, Richard C. *Animals in Islamic Tradition and Muslim Cultures*. Oxford, UK: Oneworld, 2005. 18.

[301] Berry, Rynn. *Food for the Gods: Vegetarianism and the World's Religions*. New York: Pythagorean, 1998. 244-45.

[302] Nasr, Seyyed Hossein. "Islam, the Contemporary Islamic World, and the Environmental Crisis." In *Islam and Ecology: A Bestowed Trust*, edited by Richard C. Foltz et al. Cambridge, MA: Harvard U.P., 2003. 85–106. 97.

[303] Words of the prophet Muhammed in Friedlander, Shems. *Submission: Sayings of the Prophet Muhammad*. New York: Harper Colophon, 1977. 65.

[304] Ṣaḥīḥ al-Bukhārī 3019, Ṣaḥīḥ Muslim 2241. "Hadith On Animals: Allah Rebukes a Prophet for Killing Ants." *Daily Hadith Online*. N.d. https://www.abuaminaelias.com/dailyhadithonline/2012/11/14/allah-reprimands-prophet-ants/

[305] *Qur'an 6:38*. Trans. N. J. Dawood. Harmondsworth, UK: Penguin, 1956.

[306] Foltz, Richard C. "Islamic Environmentalism: A Matter of Interpretation." In *Islam and Ecology: A Bestowed Trust*, edited by Richard C. Foltz et al. Cambridge, MA: Harvard U.P., 2003. 249–80. 254.

[307] *Mishkat al-Masabih*. bk. 6, ch. 7, 8:178. "Animals in Islam II." *Islam, the Modern Religion*. http://www.themodernreligion.com/misc/an/an2.htm).

[308] Foltz, Richard C. "Islamic Environmentalism: A Matter of Interpretation." In *Islam and Ecology: A Bestowed Trust*, edited by Richard C. Foltz et al. Cambridge, MA: Harvard U.P., 2003. 249–80. 254.

[309] Foltz, Richard C. *Animals in Islamic Tradition and Muslim Cultures*. Oxford, UK: Oneworld, 2005. 111.

[310] Haq, S. Nomanul. "Islam and Ecology: Toward Retrieval and Reconstruction." In *Islam and Ecology: A Bestowed Trust*, edited by Richard C. Foltz et al. Cambridge, MA: Harvard U.P., 2003. 121–54. 149.

[311] Esposito, John L. *Islam: The Straight Path*. Oxford: Oxford U.P., 1988. 75.

[312] Denny, Frederick M. *Islam and the Muslim Community*. San Francisco: HarperSanFrancisco, 1987. 8.

[313] Masri, Al-Hafiz Basheer Ahmad. *Animal Welfare in Islam*. Leicestershire, UK: Islamic Foundation, 2007. xi.

[314] Said, Abdul Aziz, and Nathan C. Funk. "Peace in Islam: An Ecology of the Spirit." In *Islam and Ecology: A Bestowed Trust*, edited by Richard C. Foltz et al. Cambridge, MA: Harvard U.P., 2003. 155–84. 163.

[315] Nasr, Seyyed Hossein. "Islam, the Contemporary Islamic World, and the Environmental Crisis." In *Islam and Ecology: A Bestowed Trust*, edited by Richard C. Foltz et al. Cambridge, MA: Harvard U.P., 2003. 85–106. 97.

[316] Said, Abdul Aziz, and Nathan C. Funk. "Peace in Islam: An Ecology of the Spirit." In *Islam and Ecology: A Bestowed Trust*, edited by Richard C. Foltz et al. Cambridge, MA: Harvard U.P., 2003. 155–84. 163.

[317] Foltz, Richard C. *Animals in Islamic Tradition and Muslim Cultures*. Oxford, UK: Oneworld, 2005. 88.

318 Foltz, Richard C. *Animals in Islamic Tradition and Muslim Cultures*. Oxford, UK: Oneworld, 2005. 33-35.

319 Llewellyn, Othman Abd-ar-Rahman. "The Basis for a Discipline of Islamic Environmental Law." In *Islam and Ecology: A Bestowed Trust*, edited by Richard C. Foltz et al. Cambridge, MA: Harvard U.P., 2003. 185–248. 194.

320 Masri, Al-Hafiz Basheer Ahmad. *Animal Welfare in Islam*. Leicestershire: Islamic Foundation, 2007. 32, 34.

321 Foltz, Richard C. *Animals in Islamic Tradition and Muslim Cultures*. Oxford, UK: Oneworld, 2005. 88.

322 Haque, Nadeem. "Al-Hafiz Basheer Ahmad Masri: Muslim, Scholar, Activist—Rebel with a Just Cause." *Animals in Islam*. Ed. Nadeem Haque. NY: Lantern, 2022. 59.

323 Kemmerer, Lisa. *Animals and World Religions*. Oxford: Oxford UP, 2012. 227.

324 Kemmerer, Lisa. *Animals and World Religions*. Oxford: Oxford UP, 2012. 289.

325 Cassuto, David N. "The CAFO Hothouse: Climate Change, Industrial Agriculture, and the Law." *Animals and Society Institute Policy Paper*, 2010. 4. Also see Kemmerer, Lisa. *Eating Earth: Environmental Ethics and Dietary Choice*. Oxford: Oxford U. Press, 2014. 8-11.

326 "U.S. Eats 5 Times More than India Per Capita." May 4, 2008. *Times of India*. http://timesofindia.indiatimes.com/articleshow/3008449.cms?utm_source=contentofinterest&utm_medium=text&utm_campaign=cppst. Also, see Kemmerer. *Eating Earth*. Oxford: Oxford U. Press, 2014. 9.

327 Oppenlander, Richard A. *Comfortably Unaware: Global Depletion and Food Responsibility . . . What You Choose to Eat Is Killing our Planet*. Minneapolis: Langdon Street, 2011. 12.

328 Steinfeld, Henning, et al. *Livestock's Long Shadow: Environmental Issues and Options*. Rome: Food and Agriculture Organization of the United Nations, 2006. 272.

329 Oppenlander, Richard A. *Comfortably Unaware*. Minneapolis: Langdon Street, 2011. 6. Also, see

- Kemmerer, Lisa. *Eating Earth: Environmental Ethics and Dietary Choice*. Oxford: Oxford U. Press, 2014. 14-15.
- Steinfeld, Henning, et al. *Livestock's Long Shadow: Environmental Issues and Options*. Rome: Food and Agriculture Organization of the United Nations, 2006. 82, 95, 112.

330 Wozniacka, Gosia. "The Greenhouse Gas No One's Talking About: Nitrous Oxide on Farms, Explained." *Civil Eats*. Sept. 2019. https://civileats.com/2019/09/19/the-greenhouse-gas-no-ones-talking-about-nitrous-oxide-on-farms-explained/. Also, see Kemmerer, Lisa. *Eating Earth: Environmental Ethics and Dietary Choice*. Oxford: Oxford U. Press, 2014. 16-17.

331 "Sources of Eutrophication." *World Resource Institute.* https://www.wri.org/our-work/project/eutrophication-and-hypoxia/sources-eutrophication.

332 "What Happens to Animal Waste?" *FoodPrint.* https://foodprint.org/issues/what-happens-to-animal-waste/. Also, see Oppenlander, Richard A. *Comfortably Unaware: Global Depletion and Food Responsibility . . . What You Choose to Eat Is Killing our Planet.* Minneapolis: Langdon Street, 2011. 54.

333 "Sources of Eutrophication." *World Resource Institute.* https://www.wri.org/our-work/project/eutrophication-and-hypoxia/sources-eutrophication. Also see Kemmerer, Lisa. *Eating Earth.* Oxford: Oxford U. Press, 2014. 18-22.

334 Stanley, Morgan. "Dead Zone." *National Geographic.* https://education.nationalgeographic.org/resource/dead-zone. Also "NOAA forecasts summer 'dead zone' of nearly 5.4K square miles in Gulf of Mexico: Low oxygen in water often leads to conditions where life cannot be sustained." *National Oceanic and Atmospheric Administration.* June 2, 2022. https://www.noaa.gov/news-release/noaa-forecasts-summer-dead-zone-of-nearly-54k-square-miles-in-gulf-of-mexico

335 See Kristof, Nicholas. "Our Water-Guzzling Food Factory." *The New York Times.* May 30, 2015. https://www.nytimes.com/2015/05/31/opinion/sunday/nicholas-kristof-our-water-guzzling-food-factory.htm. Also, see Schwartz, Richard. *Vegan Revolution: Saving Our World, Revitalizing Judaism.* NY: Lantern Publishing & Media, 2020. 65.

336 Schwartz, Richard. *Vegan Revolution: Saving Our World, Revitalizing Judaism.* NY: Lantern Publishing & Media, 2020. 63.

337 Butler, Rhett A. "Brazil's Forests." *Mongabay.com.* 2020. https://rainforests.mongabay.com/brazil/.

338 "Soybeans in Brazil." *Observatory of Economic Complexity.* https://oec.world/en/profile/bilateral-product/soybeans/reporter/bra.

339 "Eating Meat Causes Climate Change." *PETA: Lambs: petalambs.* https://www.petalambs.com/why-vegan-how/meat-and-the-environment/.

340 Sauven, John. "Why Meat-Eaters should Think Much More about Soil." *The Guardian.* May 16, 2017. https://www.theguardian.com/commentisfree/2017/may/16/meat-eaters-soil-degradation-over-grazing. Also, Schwartz, Richard. *Vegan Revolution.* NY: Lantern Publishing & Media, 2020. 62.

341 Kemmerer, Lisa. *Eating Earth: Environmental Ethics and Dietary Choice.* Oxford: Oxford U. Press, 2014. 30-39.

342 Courtesy of Kemmerer, Lisa. From *Eating Earth.* Oxford: Oxford U. Press, 2014. 41.

343 Kemmerer, Lisa. *Eating Earth: Environmental Ethics and Dietary Choice.* Oxford: Oxford U. P., 2014. 70-75. Also, see Schwartz, Richard. *Vegan*

Revolution: Saving Our World, Revitalizing Judaism. NY: Lantern Publishing & Media, 2020. 97.

[344] Kemmerer, Lisa. *Eating Earth:* Oxford: Oxford U. Press, 2014. 58-75.

[345] Kreutz, Liz. "The State of The Ocean Is in Peril': Inside Bay Area's Marine Mammal Center Working to Help Stranded, Starving Sea Animals." ABC 7: News: Marine Mammal Center. Sept. 2, 2019. https://abc7news.com/the-marine-mammal-center-bay-area-sausalito-nonprofit/5508656/. Also, see:

- Schwartz, Richard. *Vegan Revolution: Saving Our World, Revitalizing Judaism*. NY: Lantern Publishing & Media, 2020. 96.
- Li, Wanyee. "Global Overfishing Is Starving Penguins and Other Seabirds, Says B.C. Study." *Toronto Star: Vancouver*. Dec. 6, 2018. https://www.thestar.com/vancouver/2018/12/06/global-overfishing-is-starving-penguins-and-other-seabirds-says-bc-study.html.

[346] Kemmerer, Lisa and Bethany Dopp. "A Fishy Business." *Animals and Environment: Advocacy, Activism, and the Quest for Common Ground*. Ed. Lisa Kemmerer. Routledge, 2015. 164-68. Also, see Kemmerer, Lisa. *Eating Earth: Environmental Ethics and Dietary Choice*. Oxford: Oxford U. Press, 2014. 62-70.

[347] Myers, Ransom and Boris Worm. "Rapid Worldwide Depletion of Predatory Fish Communities." *Nature* 423.6397 (2003): 280-83. 281.(Also at https://www.nature.com/articles/nature01610.)

[348] MacKenzie, Debora. "Deep-Sea Fish Species Decimated in a Generation." *NewScientist: Health*. N.p. http://www.newscientist.com/article/dn8533-deepsea-fish-species-decimated-in-a-generation.html.

[349] MacKenzie, Debora. "Deep-Sea Fish Species Decimated in a Generation." *NewScientist: Health*. N.p. http://www.newscientist.com/article/dn8533-deepsea-fish-species-decimated-in-a-generation.html.

[350] Watson, Paul. "Tora! Tora! Tora!" *Environmental Ethics: What Really Matters, What Really Works*. Ed. David Schmidtz and Elizabeth Willott. 2nd ed. New York: Oxford, 2012. 639–43. 643.

[351] Watson, Paul. "Tora! Tora! Tora!" *Environmental Ethics: What Really Matters, What Really Works*. Ed. David Schmidtz and Elizabeth Willott. 2nd ed. New York: Oxford, 2012. 639–43. 643.

[352] Friedberg, Lionel in Schwartz, Richard. *Vegan Revolution: Saving Our World, Revitalizing Judaism*. NY: Lantern Publishing & Media, 2020. 140

[353] Kemmerer, Lisa. *Eating Earth*. Oxford: Oxford U. Press, 2014. 58.

[354] Kemmerer, Lisa. *Eating Earth: Environmental Ethics and Dietary Choice*. Oxford: Oxford U. Press, 2014. 90-138.

[355] Kemmerer, Lisa. *Eating Earth*. Oxford: Oxford UP, 2012. 108.

[356] Petruzzello, Melissa. "Animals We Ate into Extinction." *Encyclopedia Britannica*. https://www.britannica.com/list/6-animals-we-ate-into-extinction. Also, see Kemmerer, Lisa. *Eating Earth: Environmental Ethics and Dietary Choice*. Oxford: Oxford U. Press, 2014. 90-93.

357 Siegel, Kassie and Brendan Cummings. "Polar Bears: Watching Extinction in Real Time." *Bear Necessities: Rescue, Rehabilitation, Sanctuary, and Advocacy.* Ed. Lisa Kemmerer. Leiden: Brill, 2015. 53.

358 Kemmerer, Lisa. *Eating Earth: Environmental Ethics and Dietary Choice.* Oxford: Oxford U. Press, 2014. 144.

359 "Going Vegan Protects Vulnerable Humans." *PETA: Lambs: Petalambs.* https://www.petalambs.com/why-vegan-how/human-rights/.

Made in the USA
Middletown, DE
26 August 2023

37359502R00070